D0123446

Food in Tibetan Life

Rinjing Dorje

illustrated by the author

Tibetan script by
Venerable T G Dhongthong

PROSPECT BOOKS

London 1985

Copyright © Rinjing Dorje 1985

Published by Prospect Books Ltd
45 Lamont Road
London SW10 0HU

Distributed in the USA by
The University Press of Virginia
Box 3608 University Station
Charlottesville VA 22903

Designed by Philip Wills

Set in Palatino by Crypticks, Leeds, West Yorkshire
Printed and bound by Smith Settle, Otley, West Yorkshire

ISBN 0 907325 22 X (Hardback)
ISBN 0 907325 26 2 (Paperback)

I dedicate this book
to my late father
Venerable Sherab Dorje
and to my living mother
Ama Choe Gyalmo

I also offer
a special dedication and respect
to His Holiness the Dalai Lama
and to the people of Tibet

ཁ་ཟས་སྨན་དང་འདྲ་བར་རིགས་པ་ཡིས། །
འདོད་ཆགས་ཞེ་སྡང་མེད་པར་བསྟེན་བགྱི་སྟེ། །
རྒྱགས་ཕྱིར་མ་ལགས་བསྙེམས་པའི་ཕྱིར་མ་ལགས། །
མཚར་གཕྱིར་མ་ལགས་ལུས་གནས་འབའ་ཞིག་ཕྱིར། །

Understanding food to be like medicine
I will use it without desire or hate
Not for pride's sake nor in arrogance
And not for beauty but just for sustenance

a popular table prayer
by the Buddhist teacher
Nagarjuna (2nd — 3rd
centuries AD)

Notes on Spelling and Pronunciation

Tibetan is written with an alphabet based on Indian scripts, with letters that stand for separate sounds, not by using characters to represent ideas as in Chinese or Japanese. Since Tibetan script is alphabetical, it is possible to transliterate Tibetan spellings by substituting English letters for the nearest equivalent Tibetan ones.

However, Tibetan, like French, is not pronounced exactly as it is spelled. There are many silent letters, and many cases where vowels become nasalized or turn into umlauts or diphthongs because of other letters which precede or follow them. Just as you would need to know the rules of French pronunciation to be able to say a French word correctly when you read it, so too you would have to understand Tibetan pronunciation rules to speak correctly a transliterated Tibetan word. For example, the word pronounced 'lama' is spelled *bla ma*; and 'yak' is spelled *g.yag*. Among the recipes in this book, 'Boetuk' (Tibetan or dumpling soup) would come out as *Bod thug*; and 'Sham trak' (baked mushrooms) would hardly be recognisable as *Sha bsreg*!

Since I expect that you might want to be able to tell people the names of the dishes you are serving, rather than look them up in a dictionary, and perhaps that you would also rather be chewing mouthfuls of Tibetan food than chewing mouthfuls of Tibetan consonants, I have used a simple system of spelling that would give you equivalent pronunciations (at least as close as is possible in English) for how Tibetans say their words, rather than how they write them. My system of equivalent pronunciation used in the book and recipes uses the normal sounds of English letters to give you the approximate Tibetan sound. If you are familiar with the vowel sounds as pronounced in the musical scale 'do re mi fa sol la ti do', this is a good guide to the pronunciation of the Tibetan vowels. The sound for 'u' is pronounced as it is in 'soup'. The double vowel 'ae', 'oe', and 'ue' are pronounced as they would be in German ('Baedecker', 'Goethe', and 'Fuehrer').

If you are interested in the Tibetan spellings, you can find them in the Glossary, where the Tibetan words are transliterated according to the Wylie system, the system most widely used at present by Tibetan scholars.

Foreword

༄༅། བོད་ཀྱི་དཔེ་མཛོད་ཁང་།

library of tibetan works and archives
GANGCHEN KYISHONG, DHARAMSALA - 176215, HIMACHAL PRADESH, INDIA

Tibetans are very innovative. Just as they borrowed their clothes from Mongolia, and their religion from India and made these things their own, so they borrowed their cuisine from China and other Central Asian countries and transformed it into something wholly Tibetan, adding it to the richness and variety of their native diet.

As will be clear from the present book, the most important ingredients of the Tibetan diet are dairy products and meat. Tibetans eat very few vegetables, which are hard to produce due to Tibet's harsh climate. So it may appear that Tibetan cooking lacks an important source of natural food; but, inasmuch as it also largely lacks the addition of spices and chemical preservatives so common elsewhere today, it can be said that Tibetan food is quite pure and natural and has nourished a robust and healthy people for centuries.

The principal staple diet of Tibetans is *tsampa*, which is common to all throughout the length and breadth of the country; indeed Tibetans and *tsampa* are almost synonymous. Whether they are at home or travelling from place to place and whether they are monks, nuns, aristocrats, farmers or nomads, wherever there is a Tibetan, there you will find *tsampa*.

Although it was common for the aristocratic elite to be provided with a rich spread of sumptuous and varied dishes, in general Tibetan cuisine is simple and easy to prepare and full of natural goodness.

The author, Mr Rinjing Dorje, is to be commended for compiling this book, which is first of its kind and invites the world at large to enjoy another unexplored aspect of Tibetan life. I hope that through reading this book people may not only learn a great deal about the ways and customs of Tibetans, and among them their cooking traditions, but may also be able to cook many of these delicious dishes themselves, by following the carefully prepared recipes in the latter part of the book.

Gyatsho Tshering
Director

NOTE
The above foreword was kindly provided as a result of the author submitting the draft of his book to:

ཉུ་འབྲེལ་ཡིག་ཚང་༎

OFFICE OF HIS HOLINESS THE DALAI LAMA

The author wishes to express his deep appreciation of the consideration thus shown for his work.

Contents

Preface

Food and cookery are an important part of the life and culture of all peoples, including Tibetans. This aspect of a culture cannot be covered by just a collection of recipes, nor by a description of foodstuffs without a detailed explanation of what is done to them. When I decided to write this book, I saw that it would have to have two parts: first description and secondly recipes.

This arrangement corresponds to the words of the title, words which were carefully chosen: 'Food in Tibetan Life'. The book is not just for cooks, but for all those many people, Tibetan and non-Tibetan, who are interested in Tibetan culture and who would be happy to have more information about this fundamental element in it.

Since one of my main purposes in writing the book is to reveal and share my understanding of ordinary Tibetans and their way of life, I feel obligated to state my credentials and background as a Tibetan. I spent part of my childhood in the village of Shabru, which is now on the Nepalese side of the border but used to be in Tibet, and part in southern Tibet. People there lived partly as farmers and partly as nomads, so I gained experience of both these important and traditional Tibetan ways of life. It is these which I describe in the book, often in the present tense although I know that much has changed in Tibet since my childhood.

Our unique and centuries old culture is now carried on by only a small number of Tibetans, outside the country, under the guidance of His Holiness the Dalai Lama. Since the invasion of Tibet by the People's Republic of China in 1950 this culture has been in danger of being lost to the world. But, even though many of the best parts of our way of life have been destroyed in our homeland, some of us continue to practise and enjoy them in exile. I hope that those who read this book will also gain from it some 'taste' and appreciation for the true Tibetan life-style.

For this purpose I have been careful to choose recipes which are authentically Tibetan. Of course, the cookery of any people reflects influences from outside. This may be less true of Tibet than of countries in regions like Europe, but it is still true. A comprehensive picture of Tibetan food must include some dishes which have come from, say, Nepal or China. So I have also recorded a selection of these, in the Appendix, separate from the ones which I consider to be 100% Tibetan.

I have also been careful to describe the recipes as they would be made in Tibet. During the last ten years of living in the United States my wife and I have been regularly preparing our native food. We have found that all the ingredients we need are available, except for a few things like yak meat, dri's milk and one or two spices. We have been satisfied with substitutes for these, and I explain this in the recipes. So readers can cook and taste foods just like those eaten in Tibet.

Acknowledgements
I could not have written this book without help from these special people. First of all, I would like to thank my wife Yeshe Dolma, who assisted me in perfecting every recipe in it. And we would both like to thank our children Guru and Dewa who have brought happiness and satisfaction to our lives. Special thanks are also due to those friends who contributed time and effort to helping me with English writing style and editorial assistance: Ter Ellingson and Larry Epstein. I also thank Geshe Nornang, who contributed some of the recipes; and the Venerable T G Dhongthong for writing the words in Tibetan script for me. I am grateful to Philip Wills and Soun Vannithone for the improvements they made to my own drawings.

Finally, I am most thankful to my longtime friend David Hoffman of Dorje Ling Publishing, who published my first book, *Tales of Uncle Tompa*, and has encouraged me in writing more; and to Alan and Jane Davidson and all at Prospect Books for fully sharing my concept of the present volume and working in friendship with me to bring it into print.

Rinjing Dorje
Seattle, Washington, USA

Tibetan year of 'Wood-mouse'
1984

Land and People

The country of Tibet has been isolated for centuries behind the great wall of the Himalayas. Tibet covers a vast land area and to cross the country by caravan, as many Tibetans did, takes about four months of steady walking.

Tibet is a high land with many mountains and valleys, and many different regions and dialects. The culture of Tibet is ancient, and her people lived in happiness and contentment for many centuries.

The people of Tibet numbered about six million when I was a child. If I describe them in the present tense, despite changes which have afflicted their way of life, this is because aspects of that way of life undoubtedly survive and it would not be natural for me to refer to everything I remember as though it was gone for ever. Most Tibetans are followers of Buddhism, and there are many monks and nuns. There are also artisans, traders, and craftspeople; but most of the ordinary people are either farmers or nomads who herd animals. Among these people there are rich and poor. A farmer used to be counted rich if he owned several fields and some livestock. The more of each he had, the richer he was. Traders were counted rich when they had many donkey- or mule-loads of goods to trade. A man was also considered rich if his wife wore a lot of jewelry, or if he could afford more than one wife and both wore jewelry.

The daily life of most Tibetans was and no doubt remains fairly simple. They depend on the few foods that they can grow or trade, but they also use some foods that do not come from Tibet. Foods such as tea, brown sugar, rice, corn, spices, and dried fruit have traditionally been brought in from the neighbouring countries of India, Nepal, and China. Dried fruits like raisins are considered a luxury food and would be used to prepare for holiday celebrations, not for everyday eating. But tea is used every day and indeed many times every day.

Tibetans sometimes use money, especially in the larger towns and Lhasa, but they usually trade for goods. Wool and musk are both trade items. Sometimes they trade rare herbs that only grow in the high mountains. One 'herb' that is highly valued for trade is *yartsa gumbu*. *Yar* means summer; *tsa* means grass; *gum*, winter; and *bu*, insect. In the summer this is a plant, but it is believed that its root becomes an insect in the winter. People go out to collect it on winter days with no wind. See the drawing on page 14. They know that a small plant which trembles slightly when there is no wind has an insect at its root. (Really, the plant is a fungus of the genus *Cordyceps*, which does grow on insects or their larvae but kills them in so doing.)

Looking for yartsa gumbu

To keep warm in the cold climate the people wear warm clothes made from sheepskin or thick fabric. Home-made, thick, woolen clothes are most common. The women usually weave the fabric, and the men do the spinning or help with it. They can spin with a hand-made spindle while they are traveling or herding animals. Each family weaves its own cloth, and the colors come from plants and other natural dyes.

The men generally wear darker colors and the women brighter ones; but they both usually wear shades of blue, green, or black. Dark red, orange, and yellow are religious colors. When an ordinary person wears one of these, it means that he or she has taken a religious vow or is the child of a lama. The monks and nuns usually wear dark red robes.

A woman who wears a five-colored apron is married. There are a number of other traditional ways to show that a woman is married, depending on the region of the country. In eastern Tibet, Kham, a woman wears coral, turquoise, and amber beads braided into her hair. The only sign that I know of that sometimes shows a man is married is a ring.

Most men wear knives and a sewing-needle container, and some people carry a *naru* (snuff-box). Nomad men also carry a slingshot in their belts. These are woven out of yak tail hair. They are about six feet long, woven like a rope, with a pocket in the middle. A rock is put into this pocket, and the rope is folded into two. Then it is held by the two ends, swung in a circle over the head, aimed, and one end let go. The slingshot can be very accurate if the person who throws is well practised.

Bathing is not very common in Tibet, especially during the colder parts of the year. A person might just take one bath in a whole year. Some people do not bathe at all, and older people sometimes say that taking a bath washes away all the good-fortune *yang*. Everyone washes his hair at least once a month, though. Except for the monks and nuns, both men and women wear their hair long. A small root vegetable called *sukpa* (*Lychnis* sp.) is crushed by pounding and mixed with a little water to be used as a soap for hair, and it works very well.

People do wash their faces and hands every day. Each morning, before anything is done, people get up and wash. Then they will place fresh water in the bowls before the altar as an offering. They light the butter lamp, burn incense, and say prayers. Then it is time to begin the day.

Farmers and Nomads

Not many kinds of fruit or vegetable can grow in Tibet, because the climate is too cold and dry in many places. Most of the people still live on animals like yaks and sheep and their products. Where nothing but grass grows, the people are nomads who tend animals. They eat mostly meat, and trade their animal products to farmers for dried vegetables, grains, flour, spices, and other necessities.

The farmers live in the valleys, where it is warmer. They grow grain — barley, wheat, and buckwheat — and vegetables like potatoes, turnips, daikons, radishes, onion, red chili peppers, and cilantro (coriander). They also collect wild greens, wild onions and herbs for spices, and mushrooms too. In southern valleys, where the warmth is greatest, the farmers can also grow red beans, various fruits, and rice.

Farmers have their work, and nomads have their work. The farmers depend on rain for irrigation, and often use irrigation channels from streams that come down from the high mountains. Since most farmers get only one crop a year, they also maintain livestock, which are kept down in the valley during the winter, where they fertilize the farmers' fields. By the end of the first lunar month (the end of March), farmers are at work plowing their fields with a pair of yaks or oxen, in order to mix the manure in with the soil.

By the end of the second and the beginning of the third month, the fields will be plowed again. This time the man plows and his wife follows. She carries a big basket of grain in one hand, and she sprinkles the seed on the ground with her other hand. Then men and women of the village follow them with hoes and cover up the seeds. They usually sing songs or say prayers together as they work. The elder ones say prayers more often than the young ones do. Helping others out when they need it is called 'lending hands'. It is the common practice in the villages of Tibet.

Different crops are planted according to the location of the village. In my village, Shabru, we first sow buckwheat and potatoes. In the beginning of the fourth month we plant wheat, barley, turnips, daikon, radishes, various beans, mustard, and other crops. In the lower parts of the valley they also sow millet. Late in the fifth month we plant onions, garlic, scallions, and some other vegetables.

The potatoes are weeded and resoiled around the beginning of the seventh month. Men and women and even small children go into the fields with little hoes. They carefully dig around the plants and pile more soil up over the roots. The same thing is done for the radishes, beans, and other vegetables.

The eighth and ninth months are probably the busiest of all. They start to harvest the buckwheat, wheat, and barley. The men and women stand in rows. Each grabs a handful of the stalks in one hand and cuts it with a sickle. They try to cut as close to the ground as possible. As they go along they make piles of the stalks, and these are later laid out to dry. Then they all go and thresh the stalks with flails — long sticks with rotating end pieces. This separates the straw from the grains. The straw is fed to the livestock as hay. Then the grain is put into a large woven bamboo or wickerwork tray that is flat and round. The tray is raised and shaken to allow the chaff to blow away while the grains remain. This is how we winnow the grain.

In the ninth month we also harvest the potatoes, radishes, beans, and other vegetables. These we mostly slice and dry, either to keep for the winter or to trade with the nomads for their products.

A man eating a simple meal while herding yaks

Where grains and vegetables are plentiful, people eat hardly any meat. This is because Buddhism does not allow taking the life of another. But for those, in many parts of the country, who have to eat meat for survival, one feels: 'It's permitted, for the sake of one's survival.' Thus, even though nomads have to get much of their food by slaughtering animals from their herds, their way of life is still religiously respectable. And people who live in other ways, even monks and nuns, welcome the dairy and meat products that the nomads provide.

Still, Tibetans do not eat the meat of small animals. Since a life is a life, no matter what size, people consider it better to take just one life, of a single large animal. It would take the lives of many small animals to produce as much meat.

Many Tibetans only eat the meat of animals that have hooves or horns; so do not eat fish, pork, and poultry. However, in some parts of the country people do eat these. I have yet to learn the reason for this. It is just so.

In one way or another everyone's life in Tibet depends on animals. Horses are used for traveling because the country is too rough for wide roads and carts. Donkeys are used for transporting goods. Yaks are used for meat and for transportation; also for plowing and many other things. Sheep and goats are also used for meat, wool, skin, milk, and even transportation.

Dairy products are very important as food in Tibet, and the *dri* (female yak) is used just for milk. There are also *dzos* and *dzomos* (male and female), a cross between a yak and a lowland cow. A *dzomo* does not produce as much milk as a *dri*, but the milk is sweeter and highly valued. Farmers always try to have one or two *dzos* to work in their farms. There are also cows and oxen — cows for milk, oxen for plowing.

Nothing is wasted from the livestock when they are alive, or even when they are butchered. *Tsilu*, the fat of an animal, is commonly used for frying. The fat is gathered when the animal is slaughtered, and stuffed into a stomach taken from a dead sheep, which is still very wet. When the stomach dries, it becomes hard. Then this bag of fat is hung over the stove to smoke and dry, or is hung outside to dry in the air.

Even the hair and dung of an animal can be used. The hair is used to weave fabric, and the dung makes the fields fertile again every year and is essential fuel for cooking in the areas where wood is scarce. Only the dung of animals that eat grass and leaves burns well enough to be used for cooking. Dung is especially used as fuel in the central, eastern, and northern parts of Tibet, where wood is very rare. The wet dung is put on rocks to dry. When it is put into the fire, it smells like burning herbs. The dung of larger animals is used for cooking. Sheep or goat dung is used more for heating, but most people do not have any special heating system. They just heat their houses while cooking and wear warm clothes all the time.

There are two breeds of dog that I know of in Tibet. One is called *gokhi*, which means 'entrance dog'. These dogs are very big and long-haired with big bushy tails, and they are very strong. They can also be very vicious and are used mostly by nomads. A *gokhi* wears a specially made steel spiked collar and is usually tied up with a thick chain. But at night they are let loose, and then they bark and guard the livestock.

A nomad woman making butter

The other type of dog is called *apso*, and it is strictly a pet. *Apsos* are small, with long hair and flat noses. They are very sensitive and bark a lot. The smallest ones are considered the best, and they require a lot of care. They are not common at all among the nomads and farmers. The noble families and town people of central and southern Tibet keep them.

Because the life of nomads depends totally on their livestock — yaks, sheep, *dzo* and *dzomos*, and cows as well as work animals such as horses and dogs — its pattern is very different from that of farm work: no plowing, no sowing, and no weeding. During the three or four months of winter the nomads move their animals down into the valleys, where they hope to find a little warmth and shallow snow so that the animals can dig for grass. As it gets warmer, they move to the upper parts of the mountains or onto the northern plains. They take their dairy and other animal products (meat, cooking fat, wool, etc), along with rugs which they have woven in the winter months. Then, in the ninth month, they take their products and go to *lotsong*, the annual bazaar.

The farmers also load their animals up with packs of their grain, dried vegetables, potatoes, mushrooms, and many other things and go to the bazaar. The women and children stay home to store food and get ready for the winter.

Markets and Towns

Lotsong, the annual bazaar, takes place all over Tibet from the end of the ninth month of the year to the middle of the tenth. It is very important to the lives of the ordinary people, because it is the only time of the year when nomads and farmers exchange their goods and get what they need for the whole year to come. It is also the time when traders bring foreign goods, and when all the craftsmen can sell their wares and get what they need in exchange. The bazaar is usually held somewhere in the border areas between the land of the farmers and the territory of the nomads. On average there is a bazaar for every five or six villages; but there are also bigger ones with more variety of goods and foodstuffs available. The bazaar lasts about two to three weeks.

People who come with something to trade set up little tents and put their goods out in front. They seldom use currency, but barter goods. To measure grain or *tsampa* (see recipe, page 62), we use something called a *bo*. This is a deep wooden vessel that holds approximately five pounds. For liquids and fine powdery stuff, we use something similar to a *bo*, but more tightly constructed and leak-proof.

For general weighing purposes we use a measure called a *sang* or *pulu*. This is a piece of stick that has a leather loop in the middle, allowing it to be used as a scale. One end of the stick has a leather strip with a metal hook hanging from it; the other end has a round stone tied on with a leather strap. This strap can slide along the stick, and the side of the stick that has the stone also has numbers carved into it. The stone serves as a weight. If someone wants to buy *tsilu*, for example, or *mar* (butter) he hooks it onto the metal hook. Then he takes a tight hold of the loop in the middle, lifts this up, and moves the leather strap with the stone back and forth to determine the weight by looking at the number which the leather covers when the two sides balance.

For fabrics we use a measure called *tru*, or cubit. This is the distance from the end of your middle finger to your elbow.

Every buyer and seller has his own measuring devices, such as *bo*, *pulu*, *sang*, and so on. This ensures the honesty of the measurements. The seller normally does the measuring, but the buyer has to agree before they exchange goods.

Many times buyer and seller will ask older persons to help measure.

Because of their many years of experience, they can often just tell by looking or feeling. Many things are estimated in this way, by feeling and judging, by weighing or by looking, perhaps even by listening.

Some things are measured by the handful, or even by the thumbnail. We also use spoons, cups, and spatulas to measure.

Bargaining is very common; indeed nothing is ever settled without a good bargaining session. And, of course, everyone wants to make as good a bargain as he can.

All kinds of artisans and craftspeople bring their wares to the bazaar. There are blacksmiths, silversmiths and goldsmiths, coppersmiths, and shoemakers. Because these skills and professions are almost always passed down from father to son, these people are often members of an occupational clan. So, for instance, there may be a clan of copper workers or blacksmiths. Alongside them, however, will be some people whose parents followed other occupations, but who have themselves now chosen these ones. There are also likely to be traders who have brought goods over long distances, on the backs of their animals. So the bazaar is full of all kinds of goods and people, and is a lively and interesting distraction from everyday life. People can see other people and goods from the outside world, and enjoy socializing with neighbors and friends.

In Tibet there are many small villages, bigger villages, and towns; and then there is Lhasa, the capital of the country. Lhasa is a city of large two- or three-storey houses made of brick and stone. There are also temples and monasteries, and above the city is the Potala, which was the palace of His Holiness the Dalai Lama. There are many more monasteries and nunneries in the countryside around Lhasa.

Traditionally, many different kinds of people have lived in Lhasa: Chinese, Nepalese, Indians, Bhutanese, and others. Unlike the towns and villages, Lhasa has a year-round market where traders, nomads, farmers, and all kinds of craftsman bring their products to sell, and buy what they need. Currency is in general use there, and barter is less common. The people of Lhasa are as religious as any other Tibetans, but they are also considered more clever. They make money by buying from one trader and selling to another. In this way they make a profit as middlemen and are able to support themselves in the city.

Because there is a market all year round, people of Lhasa also have more variety of food than do people elsewhere in Tibet. But the Tibetans in Lhasa grow some vegetables in their backyards too. There has for long been a Chinese influence in Lhasa — in the names of vegetables, the recipes, even in the names of pots and pans. There were also influences from Indian, Nepalese, Muslim, and other cultures. Nevertheless, Lhasa remained unmistakably Tibetan, although with more of a cosmopolitan flavor than other parts of Tibet.

Cooks and Butchers

Among the families of the ordinary people the women are the cooks. But, of course, in monasteries the cooks are men, and the professional cooks are also men. Noble or rich families would probably have a man to cook for them. These cooks are called *gyal se machem* or the master cooks. They acquire their mastery with food by working with other masters at first. It takes years of training and work as an assistant cook before they can qualify as master cooks. These master cooks are normally found in the larger towns and Lhasa, not in the villages. A master cook is hired for wedding parties, special ceremonies that can last for days, or any large banquet. In Tibet this is considered a good skill to acquire, and anyone who wants to do so can join a master cook as his assistant and learn it.

Occupations in Tibet may be determined either by personal choice or by what profession your parents and grandparents practised. Trades and skills are passed on within a family from parents to children. Blacksmiths, butchers, shoemakers, and beggars are considered low class, and a person belonging to one of these categories usually only marries someone else from the same class. But in Tibet this is not a rule that would lead to punishment if someone broke it. Even people from a low class seem to be quite as happy as everyone else. After all, they are very important for the daily lives of everyone in the villages and towns. They know how much they are needed.

There is an old legend about how one particular butcher clan named *Shempa Marutsepa* came into being. Marutsepa lived a long time ago, and was a butcher by trade. He did not particularly like to slaughter animals, but that was how he made his living and supported his family.

One day he took a herd of lambs up into the mountains to butcher them. It was the custom to take the animals away from the village before slaughtering them. It was also the custom to bind the animals' feet before cutting their throats. While Marutsepa was busy going around doing this, one lamb picked up Marutsepa's butchering knife and hid it clumsily in the dirt. Then the lamb lay down on top of the knife and started to weep.

Marutsepa saw the lamb crying, which was a very unusual thing for an animal to do. He went over and took the lamb in his arms. Then he saw the knife handle sticking up out of the dirt. In a shock he recognized that the animal was like a human being and did not want to die. But it had no voice to speak with.

Marutsepa felt such a sharp regret that he decided he could no longer live by killing. He freed all the animals and then jumped from a high cliff. His family found his body and brought it home.

It is the custom in Tibet to place the body in a sitting position in the house, near the family altar while they call in a lama to perform religious rites. It is kept there for either twenty-one or forty-nine days while the family performs all the proper funeral ceremonies. The body is disposed of when these rites are completed; they will take anything from a few to forty-nine days depending on the family astrologer's computations.

Marutsepa with the lamb which aroused his compassion

The next day, as Marutsepa's family was performing the ceremonies, his body miraculously came to life again. He had discovered the wisdom of the Buddha's compassion and become enlightened. Since that time, it is said that any animal butchered by one of Marutsepa's clan is always transferred to a better existence in its next life.

There are others who are not members of this clan or of any butcher clan who must also slaughter animals in order to survive. This is especially true among the nomads, who are often far from towns and regular butchers. Before an animal is butchered prayers are said for the animal and it is given water that has been blessed. A butter lamp is also put in front of the altar as an offering before the animal is killed.

Religion, Monasteries and Nunneries

Religion is the center of everyone's life in Tibet. When not talking or laughing, many people pray as they work all day long. There is a close relationship and many family and friendship ties between the monks and nuns and the lay people. Besides such personal ties monks and nuns also perform many kinds of religious services for lay people. For example a lama or monk who spends his entire life in a monastery will pray when a farmer's animal has to be butchered. He does this to help the animal attain a better rebirth in its next life.

Monks and nuns also might perform other, not necessarily religious, services for lay people. In southwestern Tibet there is a region called Kyirong, 'Happy Valley', not far from my home. Youngsters from there would go to a monk called Gen Rigzin, who lived in a cave up on the mountain of Happy Valley. They went there to learn reading and writing from him. He was also known to be an expert on grammar, poetry, and the general philosophy of Buddhism. Yet he lived a very simple life with his sister, who took care of him. He taught the youngsters with his love and compassion. This was one of the ways these youngsters became educated. As this went on, it became just like a summer camp for them.

Another kind of service used to be offered by the nuns of Pashing Gonpa, a nunnery where the nuns ran a water mill. This mill was not for grinding grain for flour, but was used to make wooden bowls and cups for sale. They made all kinds of wooden kitchen containers.

This water mill was built just like a little house near a river. In the bottom of the house, as the drawing shows, there was a large turning wheel with many wooden square paddles attached. A large wooden sluice canal led a stream of water down from the river above. Water shot down forcefully through the canal, and then hit the paddles in the bottom of the house. The force of the water turned the main wheel. The metal shaft from the water wheel was connected to a lathe on the floor above. On this floor there was a box frame built to fit different sizes of logs. Each of the turning wheels in the frame had attached to it router blades. These blades were made in different shapes to cut and carve different items, and the nuns changed the blades depending on what they were making. Template shapes were cut in the router frame, to guide the wood blocks against the blades for a perfect cut every time. A sluice gate at the river end was used either to divert water into the system, or to shut the mill down for rest or repairs.

These nuns used to spend most of the time in their religious activities, but they also put some time into their factory production. It appears that mostly young nuns worked on this mill, rather than the elders. I also remember that some ran the mill, and some did the painting and drawing on the bowls, while some polished them and still others did the packing and got them ready to sell. So it seems that Tibetan nuns, just like Henry Ford in America, had discovered the idea of the factory assembly line. In fact, these nuns were so inventive that they had even constructed a wooden automatic robe lifter for the nunnery outhouse (w.c.).

Monasteries in Tibet such as those around Lhasa often have, or had, thousands of monks living in them, sometimes as many as ten thousand in one monastery. There are huge kitchens with pots so big that they are like small rooms. These pots are never moved from the

The nuns' water mill

big stoves and are stirred with paddles that are like boat oars. Monks use ladders to climb down into the pots when the time comes to clean them.

These pots are mostly used for tea, and it is said that some require heating for twenty-four hours to get the water hot enough. Big scoops are used to pour the tea from the big pot into the churns. After the butter and the salt are added, two monks stand opposite each other and churn the tea. The churn is then tipped sideways, and tea is poured into large teapots. Young monks carry these teapots around and pour tea into the cups of the monks who are sitting in rows and chanting.

Astrologers, Weathermakers and Healers

Most Tibetans depend on astrology for all important events or decisions. Marriages are mostly arranged, but you do have an opportunity to tell your parents if you are in love. Then they will have an astrological chart made up for the two of you. If you don't match — no marriage! Your parents will then have to go out and look around for another bride or groom to match you; and this is not an easy task for the parents.

Many other kinds of decisions are made using astrology: building a house, travelling, moving to another place, choosing a day for a special ceremony. Sometimes even the right days and times for spring plowing and planting are determined by astrology. Astrologers study for years and years. They are very skilled in their subject, and have to pass difficult examinations. Word of their accuracy spreads quickly through the community, establishing their reputations.

Some hermits spend their lives meditating in caves so that they can learn to control the weather for farmers. These hermits are called *lahtso* (singular, *lah*). In the farming regions of the country, every few villages will have a *lah*. The *lah* often spends six months in retreat, practising his spiritual power to control the weather for the next six months.

There are old stories that tell how hermits are judged to be qualified as *lahtso*. A lama calls all the hermits together after they have been in retreat. In front of the entire village the lama puts a sieve down into a big vat of water. As the lama lifts the sieve above his head, he instructs one of the hermits to keep the water from running out of it. The hermit has to say his mantras (powerful religious phrases) and completely stop the water. Then the lama may ask him to release the water, and he does so accordingly. This testing may go on for some time before the lama judges the hermit worthy to be any of the various kinds of 'spiritual layman', including the *lah*.

Lahtso are usually quite well off. They make a good living when the weather goes well, because each farmer gives a part of his harvest to the *lah* of his village. But when the weather is bad and the rains do not come as they should, the farmers may begin to distrust the *lahtso*, who may then have to leave that part of the country and take up their work elsewhere.

Most people believe that almost all illness is caused by displeasing the gods or goddesses, or else by demons, ghosts, witches and Nagas. They believe nothing will go wrong as long as one keeps every one of these beings happy. Even lamas and spiritual healers teach this, though the philosophers in Tibet say that most illnesses are created by one's own mind. They believe that if the mind can create illness, it can heal as well.

There are spiritual healers and herbal or ayuvedic physicians. A lama who is a spiritual healer does a special kind of divination for the patient. The patient explains his problem and the lama asks for his name, age, and other personal information, then performs his prayers and mantras, and meditates. Next he either counts his rosary or, in some cases uses a pair of dice. He looks to see if the number comes up odd or even. Then using a special number system he opens his scriptures and looks through them until he comes to the patient's problem.

The lama can generally accurately tell about how, when, and in what circumstances the problem was caused. Then he advises the patient either to see a physician or to worship the specific gods or goddesses who caused his sufferings or ones who can help to cure it. Some lamas are all three — spiritual healer, physician, and spiritual chart maker. My father, the Venerable Sherab Dorje, was one of these.

There are many ways to heal oneself, whether the sickness is caused by one's own psychological suffering or is an externally caused disease or accident. And sometimes a *lhaba* will be called up to heal a sick person. After reciting certain mantras and blowing over the diseased area, he will use his mouth to suck the poisons out of the system. Even solid pieces are often brought out this way. Also we have *megyapa*, a form of moxibustion, which works by burning certain plant materials on the skin. Acupuncture is also practised, except that in Tibet we use a red hot rod about the size of a pencil which is burned into the body at any one of 84 different locations depending upon the disease.

Tibetans have their own natural ways of healing that they have practised for centuries. Even when there is no physician or spiritual healer nearby, people still manage to help themselves. Nature seems to provide every medicine needed for illness, once one can discover and understand the proper methods of using these cures.

There are simple things in Tibetan medicine that are very important. Musk is one of these. When mixed with water and taken, it reduces fever. When applied to the skin it works to heal cuts and wounds and any kind of external injury. A bear's gallbladder works in the same way for injuries. There are also plants, flowers, roots, barks, fruits, and buds used for healing. Many parts of animals and birds are used as medicines for different illnesses.

For instance, I have seen a patient with a stomach ulcer treated with the stomach of an eagle. When a person suffers from stress, anxiety, and heart weakness, he or she is treated with the heart blood of a *drong* (wild yak). The blood must be taken under certain conditions: on the night of a full moon when the patient is totally calm and no noise interferes. The patient eats about half a teaspoon of the blood, and one bowl of *chang* (see recipe, p 54).

An interesting study of Tibetan medicine has been published by the Wellcome Institute of the History of Medicine. It is by the Venerable Rechung Rinpoche. People who are interested can learn a lot from it.

Men and Women

The warm feelings between young men and women are the same in Tibet as everywhere else. It is human nature. Each sex tries to attract the opposite one. For example, a young man will wear his hair long and neatly braided. He may wear gold or silver earrings and nice, clean clothes. Young women will respond to this man; and they will do similar things to make themselves attractive. Giving gifts is another way to attract someone.

Girls and boys can meet secretly wherever possible — up in the mountains while herding animals, or when the girl is sent to the mill to grind flour, etc. But there is no holding hands or kissing in public. This is considered shameful, especially if you are not married. In Tibet these acts are kept very personal.

Among the farming and nomadic communities there is a common practice that allows the young people to meet. In the winter, the boys and girls take a basketful of raw wool and say that they are going out to sit around the fire and spin it. They start a big fire outside and the boys get into one group and the girls get into another. Then they sing songs back and forth, and each group has a song leader.

The songs start up with one sex teasing the opposite sex. Each song lasts for four sentences, then the other group takes over. Sometimes the songs contain gossip, or are in verse. A song with a nice sound can become quite popular, and everyone in a village will sing it for a while. Boys and girls communicate their feelings for each other through the songs, and can offer compliments to each other. Then they may begin to get together and hold hands, and they may fall in love.

When people get married there is always a big celebration. Usually, marriage in Tibet is between one man and one woman, but some rich men can afford two wives. In some parts of the country two or more brothers may marry one woman. They do this in order to maintain their inheritance.

This does not usually cause problems as it might elsewhere. The brothers share the wife, and she is very well respected. The brothers take turns being with their wife. One will leave his shoes outside her door so the other brother will know he is with her.

Boys dancing round a fire in the winter — only one girl is shown, but see the preceding page for what happens next

8

Old and Young

Older people are greatly respected in Tibet. The older a person is, the more respect this person receives. Even someone a few years older is treated with respect. Elderly people serve as advisors to younger people. There is a saying 'the advice of an elder is more powerful than the strength of youth'. Tibetans believe this; but sometimes this proverb is used as a reminder to someone who ignores the advice of an elderly person.

Parents are very devoted to their children. Tibetans believe that children are reincarnated from previous lives, and in these earlier lives those who are now children were then the parents of us who are the parents now. Therefore it is believed we must treat our children with respect. Likewise children in Tibet are brought up to respect their parents and to think of their families before they think of themselves.

A baby is considered to be a person as soon as it is conceived in the womb. Many women can naturally feel the conception, and the baby is counted as nine months old when the mother gives birth. Possibly as soon as three days after its birth, the baby is taken to a high lama for purification rites. Then the lama gives a name to the newly born child. The mother always takes care of the child when it is a baby.

The mother carries the young baby with her wherever she goes. The baby is wrapped in a large soft shawl and is carried on the mother's back. A child is given nicer, softer clothes and better food than others; and even a beggar on the street would rather go hungry than discomfort his child.

Special ceremonies are performed for the child at the ages of three, six, nine, and twelve years. These times are believed to be astrologically important, and the child is thought to need extra protection and guidance. As early as three or four years of age, the parents start to teach children their main survival skills or ways to make a living. Trades are inherited in this way from the parents. Boys learn the skills of their fathers, and girls learn the arts of cooking, weaving, sewing, and knitting. They also learn how to handle all the family business. Tibet is known as the only country in Asia where men and women share social and family rights equally. This is quite true, and no decision is made unless the women of the family approve it.

The children get together every day and play. For toys they use whatever they can find such as rocks, pieces of wood, dirt, even the hooves and knuckle bones of animals are used as toys. The children build little temples or make tents; they make little houses out of rocks or mud or little dolls from scraps. Children are children no matter where they are, and they are full of energy and eager to learn and explore new things.

In Tibet the parents always try to teach their children to respect each other and to love peace, truth, and honesty. They also teach them to respect their elders. Parents try to offer the best of what society has.

Except for classes in the monasteries, nunneries and private tutoring, and institutions like Gen Rigzin's summer camp school (see p 26), there are no schools for children to learn to read and write. Therefore, many Tibetans are not literate. In a few villages there may be a tutor who teaches reading and writing and maybe some arithmetic, but Tibet has no tradition of schools such as exist in western countries, and the usual way for a child to get educated is to join a monastery or nunnery, and many children are taken to become monks or nuns by their parents. If the children remain at home, a boy as young as six years old takes over some or even all the responsibility of herding the family animals, and a girl of the same age can do some of the cooking for her family.

In a village, one of the worst things that could happen is for an unmarried woman to get pregnant. It is believed that this will bring bad fortune and that unfavorable things will happen to the village, especially to the farmers. They believe this misfortune will bring hail, storms, landslides, drought, and diseases.

The only way to overcome this bad fortune is for the woman to go out of the village to give birth. When she returns, she has to take a cold shower for three consecutive days. Then lamas come and perform a purification rite. They build a large fire and burn stacks and stacks of green leaves. These come from juniper, *palu* (rhododendron), and pine trees, and they make a cloud of incense over the whole village. As the lamas sit around the fire and perform the ceremony, the mother and her child have to circumambulate the fire three times. Then the woman has to wash her hair. All the villagers attend the purification rite, and embarrassment naturally shows on the woman's face.

After the ceremony and all the hardships for the woman, she and the child are now considered purified, and they are then accepted as regular members of the village. The ceremony assures that all the local gods and goddesses are happy, and that they will not cause any destruction to the villagers, their farms, or their livestock. This ritual varies in different parts of the country.

9

Habits, Respect and Humor

Most Tibetans do not smoke, especially women, though some people sniff *natag* (snuff). *Natag* is made from finely ground tobacco, cardamon, cloves, and the fine clean ashes of juniper wood. A person will grind these ingredients for days sometimes. A small mortar and pestle are carried everywhere and grinding them becomes a habit. As a person travels, at any moment of leisure he can pull out the grinder and grind away. After it is well ground, *natag* is sifted carefully into a snuffbox or *naru*. Snuffboxes are sometimes small wooden boxes with tightly fitting lids, but most commonly they are made from a yakhorn. The wide part of the horn is cut straight and hollowed out. A small hole is made in the point, and lids made to cover both ends. Sometimes they also have very fine decorations carved or embossed on them.

When someone wants some *natag*, he simply pulls out the container and unplugs the lid from the pointed end. Then he gently taps some out in a little pile onto his thumbnail. It is sniffed in, the breath is held for a few seconds, and then it is let out through the open mouth. If one sees smoke like dust coming out of the mouth and the person's eyes are filled with tears, it is considered very good *natag*.

A person will never take snuff in front of an altar, temple, monastery, nunnery, or even in front of monks, unless the monks take snuff themselves, which some do. People also smoke pipes. These pipes resemble short walking sticks, and they are popular among the nomads.

To make a greeting, especially to those who are high lamas, incarnate lamas, officials, or even just elders, a person takes off his hat, unties his hair and folds his hands. Then he sticks out his tongue and bows. Showing your thumb means asking for a favour or saying 'Please'. Showing the little finger means something is mediocre or else really bad. When women dust their aprons and spit and clap their hands, they are driving away the bad spirits. They will do this after seeing a bad omen. I was told that when British soldiers led by Colonel Young-husband marched into Tibet in 1903, Tibetan men and women all came out of their homes and applauded the invaders. The British were pleased by this warm welcome, but now you can see the real reason why the Tibetans clapped their hands.

Tibetans believe that the body is always accompanied by five gods associated with the five elements. So taking care of yourself is not just for personal comfort, it is also pleasing to the gods. For this reason one would never walk or jump over any part of someone else's body. This would be disrespectful to the other person's gods.

Nicknames are very common in Tibet. Many of the given names in Tibetan are very common, and so one is given a nickname according to the way he or she looks or acts. Or sometimes something unusual happens to a person and she or he will get a nickname from that event.

For example, at one time I lived in a monastery and had my head shaved. It seems that the back of my head is flat so everyone at the monastery called me 'Flathead'. Besides the entertainment value, nicknames are useful in large monasteries that have thousands of monks, because so many of them have the same names.

One of our neighbors in the village was named Kusho Dungchen Na, which means 'Honorable Trumpet Nose'. His wife's name was Ribong, which means 'Rabbit'. No one in the village even knew their real names. One elderly fellow was called Yakgo, which means 'Yak-headed'. His head had once gotten badly bumped and then healed imperfectly, so that there were two lumps sticking out of his head like horns. I once asked him how he had gotten hurt. He said he once lived in a monastery and he and a few other monks got into a fight. Since the monks are not allowed to carry weapons, they use rocks or sticks, and sometimes they even use a wooden tea bowl. The edges of these bowls are rather sharp. Two monks hit him with their bowls, and the cut that he got never healed properly.

There was also a person with one eye missing. He was named Ekajati, which is the name of a goddess who has one eye in her forehead. I also knew Agu Ra, which means 'Uncle Goat'. The man with this nickname had a beard sticking out just like a goat's. Then there was Mr Shig Mathar, which means 'Even a Louse Can't Pass Through'. He had a somewhat large nose that was so sharply pointed that not even a tiny insect like a louse could climb up. Finally, there was Mr Kigyak, which means 'Dog Shit'. I have no idea how his story originated.

Although people may get nicknames in such rude ways as these, no one seems to take offense. Almost everyone gets a nickname except some high lamas and officials, who are usually treated more formally. Tibetans, though, are just naturally a very humorous people. Almost everyone knows and enjoys telling some good jokes. They like to tell dirty jokes and tease each other so that everyone can laugh and enjoy them.

In an argument the worst thing you can call a person is *nyalu* which means bastard. Another bad name is *kamar* which literally means red-mouth. In Tibet *kamar* means an orphan whose parents have both died and who has no relatives at all. The name indicates that the person ate up his parents and all his relatives, and so his mouth is still red from their blood.

No matter what part of Tibet you are in, there is always a phrase to swear you are telling the truth. The most common one is *kunchok sum*. This means 'the three precious jewels', or the Buddha, the Dharma, and the Sangha. Some people swear by calling on the names of their local gods and goddesses. Where I grew up people swore by saying *dzamling kur*. This means 'carry the whole world', or in other words, the person swears if he is not telling the truth he would carry the sins of the whole world.

Most people prefer not to swear as it is not considered a good thing to do. But such words as *kyagpa kampo* or 'dried shit' naturally slip out sometimes, no matter how hard one tries. Traders seem to swear more often than anyone else.

A Tibetan kitchen with a stone stove, as described on the next page

Homes and Kitchens

The kind of dwelling Tibetans live in depends on whether they are farmers or nomads. Nomads have heavy thick tents made from the hair of the yak. These tents come apart piece by piece so that they can be rolled up and loaded onto yaks, ponies, or *dzos*. Then when the nomads reach a new place, they can unfold them and set them up. Most of these tents take three large poles, one at each end with one going across between them to form the ceiling ridge. Rope is used to hold the side of the tent out.

In most tents there is only large room for the whole family. They use a metal tripod for a stove, which is placed in the middle of the room. One corner of the tent always has a little altar, and the opposite corner is usually where the bed for the father and mother goes. If the children are young, their bed is normally right next to that of their parents.

The houses in the villages are usually simple. The kitchen is not a separate room, just one large room that is used for cooking and dining. Foods that are needed every day are stored in small bags and hung around the kitchen. Sometimes a tripod is used for cooking. Wood is used for fuel, although animal dung is used in areas where wood is scarce. Some houses have stoves made of mud and stone. A fire is built in the middle of them for cooking. These stoves do not usually have a separate oven. Breads can be baked on the top or right in the fire-box, by pushing the fire to one side or waiting until there are just warm embers and ashes.

For light at night Tibetans use butter lamps, oil lamps, and *metang*. *Metang* is pine wood that contains a lot of sap. Normally this is the bottom part of the tree, but the thicker parts of the roots are rich in sap and light well once they are split and dried. In farming villages *menag* is also used for light. *Menag* is the exhausted part of mustard seed after the seeds are pressed for oil. The mustard seed is coarsely ground and sprinkled lightly with hot water and mixed into a dough which is stuffed into a sack. This sack goes into a wooden barrel that has a small spigot on the bottom of one side. A flat round stone or wooden board that is smaller in diameter than the barrel is put on the sack to act as a plunger, and more rocks are piled on top to press it down. The whole process is done out in the direct sun. The barrel is left in the sun for several days. As the weight presses down, mustard oil starts slowly dripping out through the spigot into the container. More and more weight is added. After straining the oil is then stored in little sheepskin bags and wooden jars. It takes at least two or three days before all the oil is pressed, depending on the quantity of the seeds being processed.

The exhausted mustard seed hulls are sometimes fed to livestock. But they can also be made into balls, put on a stick and dried. These balls on the sticks are called *menag*. Once dried, they burn well, and can also be used for light.

A press for extracting mustard seed oil

Food is stored in many different ways. Except for what is needed for everyday use, farmers keep their grains in storage rooms. There are usually small separate rooms for each foodstuff. These rooms are dark with very small windows, just big enough to let the air circulate. Poor families who do not have these rooms in their houses dig storage cellars in the ground for their foods and grains. Here they also store grain that will be used later for seeds.

Nomads keep their grain and beans in tightly woven bags and sacks of various sizes. Butter is put into sheepskins or even baby yak skin bags that have been soaked in water. These are stitched up tight, and, as the skin dries, the bags shrink and form a tight seal around the stitches and butter. This way they become waterproof and airtight, and butter can be stored in them for years.

In the farming villages, the butter used for daily consumption is kept in large water tanks. The butter floats on the top, and the evaporation of the water around the butter keeps it cool. This is especially important during the warmer summer months in the farming valleys.

The kinds of pots and utensils people use vary in different parts of the country. In the southern parts of Tibet, there are many metal pots that are brought in by traders from Nepal and India or from Eastern Tibet, where they are made. They are brought in by horse or donkey. Potmakers themselves sometimes bring their wares to sell. There are also local blacksmiths who can make pots and pans, as well as other kinds of containers.

Pots and containers are made out of clay, wood, brass, copper, bronze, or iron. Most of the bowls, teacups, scoops, and spatulas are made from wood. Many kinds of wood are used. The more convoluted and interesting the grain, the more valuable the utensil is thought to be. There is a story about a very special sort of wood that says if a cup is made from this wood, the cup can detect poison. It is called *zabya*, and it is made from a burl that grows out of the side of a particular tree. You have to go out at night to look for it, because it glows in the dark. Cups made from this are naturally very special and highly prized.

Everyone uses fire to cook, and so everyone must be able to start a fire. Among the nomads, each person carries a flint-striker. Whenever a fire is needed, the flint-striker is untied from the belt. There is a small leather wallet attached to the striker which contains a few pieces of flintstone and tinder, or *pawa*. *Pawa* is a cotton-like material gathered from thistles that grow up in the mountains. Once it is dried it catches fire very easily.

To make a fire, the *pawa* is held firmly in the left hand, together with the flintstone. The stone is on top of the *pawa*, so that the sparks fall into it. Then the fire builder grasps the steel striker in his right hand and brings it down sharply against the edge of the stone. One or two strong strokes will throw a good spark into the *pawa*, which will then catch fire. Then the *pawa* is placed in dried leaves. Next one blows on it gently to start the flames up.

In the farming villages each home has a fire that goes continuously. It is very rare for the fire to go out, though sometimes it burns down to just embers and ashes. If it does go out, someone in the family will go to their neighbors to get fire. Each family also has a flint-striker for use if needed. But the best thing is just to keep the fire going.

There is an old proverb that goes *mengul shi, jengul lang*. It means: 'when one plays with fire, it dies out; when one plays with one's penis, it rises up'. This might be told to a youngster by an older person, but more often, it would be a comment by an adult. However, it is not something that a mother would say in the family circle, as it would not be considered proper to talk like this. But, if a child needed a warning, almost anybody might say it. Roughly it means it is better to play with anything instead of fire.

Meals and Daily Life

Most people eat three times a day for regular meals, and they also have snacks. The first meal comes early in the morning. It is usually *tsamtuk* or tsampa soup, perhaps together with roasted soybeans, pieces of *chura* (dried cheese) and sometimes dried meat and *tsilu* (dried fat). Each person would have at least three bowls of this to eat. Hot buttered tea is served with the soup and each person drinks at least three or four cups of this also.

The biggest meal of the day is served at noon, and dinner is always light. Tea drinking is one of the main habits of the Tibetans. Most people drink tea all day long when they are at home. People are constantly reaching out for the oil-rich, shiny tea cups. This is especially true of the older people. Before drinking the tea, a Tibetan may gather a bit of butter floating on the top of the tea and gently rub it around his nose or behind the ears. This keeps the skin from drying out in the cold weather.

Between meals there is always something to munch on. There is *chura*, dried meat, or *yoe* (toasted or partly popped grain). More frequent meals are served if someone does more physical labor and needs to eat more.

Tibetans have their own ideas about manners and proper behavior just like people everywhere. Chewing with an open mouth is considered bad manners. Stretching out one's legs, loud chatting, spitting out the food once it is in your mouth, or starting to eat before praying are all considered bad manners. As a guest, you would not eat until the person who sits at the head of the row starts the prayers and then eats. This is usually a lama or someone who has taken a religious vow or the oldest layman present.

Once a very respected lama came to visit my father. Special food was prepared for him including some *momo* (see recipe, p 82) which had just been fried in hot oil. I was sitting close to the lama when he was served and he quickly popped a *momo* into his mouth. It must have been terribly hot, because I could hear it sizzling in his mouth. Then his eyes filled with tears, but of course he could not spit it out, because that would have been bad manners. Unfortunately for the lama, as the guest of honor he had also been served very hot buttered tea, and so when he drank this he got no relief. Poor man!

Depending on the region, sometimes a guest should nicely lick off the plate or bowl he ate from and wipe it out before getting up. If he can he should belch out loud. This is considered a sign of appreciation for the meal. But this custom varies in different parts of the country, and certainly would not be considered good manners everywhere.

When a person is eating and a second person joins him, the first person will not eat until the second one eats. Then he would offer the guest more than he has himself. It is customary in Tibet that when you are first offered food, you sincerely refuse it. Then the host will insist and insist. Finally you accept the food by saying 'Only a very little', even if you are very hungry. This custom is especially common in the central and southern parts of the country.

It is said that when the first representative from Great Britain came to Lhasa he gave a big party for all the Tibetan officials. Trays of food were brought out, but the Tibetans politely refused. Not knowing the local custom the representative then had the food taken away and it was not offered again. After that, it took the representative a long time to make friends and be welcomed in Lhasa society.

Yearly Customs and Festivals

Tibetans use a lunar calendar. This means that during the 1980s the first month of their year falls somewhere near the end of February or the beginning of March on the Western calendar. Over a period of time the position changes, because there are fewer days in the lunar calendar for every year (360) than in the solar calendar (365).

On the twenty-ninth day of the twelfth month a soup called *gutuk*, a dumpling soup similar to *boetuk* (see recipe, p 80) is served. This is the day before the thirtieth, the last day of the year, and a special celebration is held to get ready for *Losar*, New Year's Day. The celebration is held on the twenty-ninth because the thirtieth, like the fifteenth, is a holy day in Tibet.

The dumplings for *gutuk* include big ones with surprises inside, such as the objects listed below. When the soup is served in bowls, each member of the family gets one dumpling with one of these objects inside, along with other dumplings to be eaten in the normal way. Each member first opens the special large dumpling with the object inside. Whatever one finds indicates that person's personality. For instance, if a person gets:

salt	– good sign, you are all right
wool	– very lazy
coal	– malicious
chili	– rough spoken
white stone	– long life
sheep pellets	– good sign, very clever
butter	– you are very sweet and easy-going

These are the traditional objects put into the dumplings. Nowadays written messages are also included, much like fortune cookies. Everyone reads these out loud and has a good laugh.

Gutuk means ninth soup. According to custom everything has to be not less than nine. There must be at least nine ingredients in the soup, and each person must eat at least nine bowls. Everyone will insist on this, and so some clever guests bring their own small bowls along. Everyone saves a little at the end and then dumps this into a large wok. They each cut off a piece of hair, a piece of fingernail, and a piece of old clothing. These are put into the wok too. Then they clean the chimney and put the dirt in the wok. Finally they make an effigy of a person out of dough and set it in the center of the pile in the wok.

The youngsters take this out late at night and set it in the middle of a trail junction. While doing this they make as much noise as they can by shouting, ringing bells, booming guns, even beating pots and pans. This traditional ceremony is called *lue*. This is done to get rid of all the negative forces at the end of the year and get ready for a new year.

The yearly cycle starts with New Year's Day. In Tibet this is called *Losar* and it is the biggest holiday celebration of the year. Lamas and monks work hard to prepare the monasteries for the ceremony. Outside they whitewash the monastery and dust and clean on the inside. Prayer flags are hung up all around the monastery, and brand new brocades from China are put on the statues of Buddhas and other deities. Most monks also receive a new set of robes from their patrons or family.

The pots and pans are glittering clean. Fine ash soap is used to wash the pots, and some of these big pots and pans have not been washed inside and out like this for a whole year. Even the stone steps leading up to the monastery are rubbed and oiled. Hundreds of butter lamps are lit, and bundles of incense are ready to burn. Whatever flowers one can find are put on the altar, and hundreds of holywater bowls are shined up until they sparkle and filled with fresh water.

Two piles of *kapse* (see recipe, p 68) are placed in front of the altar. *Kapse* is decorated with all sorts of luxury foods such as candies, dried fruits, rock-sugar, and nuts. Outside in the courtyard of the monastery there is a large pile of juniper, rhododendron, and other fragrant branches and flowers ready to light for use as incense during the ceremony.

Among the lay people, everyone is excited about *Losar*. They too clean the house, and sometimes whitewash as well. Everything is cleaned up and made shiny. The children are the most excited of all, as many receive a new set of clothing. Sometimes they also receive sweets such as rock candy, raw sugar (*buram*), or even hardened honey. People start preparations days ahead to be ready for the New Year's celebration.

I remember I always had a hard time falling asleep on the night before *Losar*. I was very anxious to wear my new clothes in the morning and to see everything all brightened up. Even the yaks' and sheep's horns are oiled and shined. The animals wear fancy collars and new bells are put on their necks. The men and women all wash their hair and braid it. They put on their jewelry and their very best clothes.

Early on *Losar* morning, the first day of the first month of the year, even before it gets light enough for anyone to see the lines on their palms, the adult men and women walk silently to the stream or lake where the villagers normally get their daily water. Along with their large water buckets, they carry bells, and cymbals. They fill up the buckets and carry them on their backs. As they walk home they ring the bells and play cymbals. The sound is like a big herd of animals coming home. When they arrive at the house, the grandmother and grandfather of the house bring out fresh butter in a large bowl, and take a pinch of it, and stick some on, right above the forehead of each member of the family.

Then everyone else gets dressed and goes into the house and sits down in a row. The oldest person in the family sits in the place of honor, at the top of the row of seats, next to the altar. The mother or grandmother of the family brings in the *chemar* (*tsampa* mixed with butter and sugar) and passes it around. Each member of the family takes a pinchful and throws it into the air along with prayers. They do this three times and eat the fourth pinch. This is to symbolize plenty for the grain harvest in the year to come. Next each member of the family is served with a bowl of yoghurt. This symbolizes a plentiful supply of products from the animals in the year to come. Since most Tibetans are either farmers or nomads, these prayers are very important.

Each person next receives a *derka*, a plate of *kapse* along with other treats. Everyone gets exactly the same amount of *derka*, even the unborn baby in its mother's womb is given a *derka*, which is saved.

Then the *cha* (butter tea, see p 53) is served to everyone. The mother and daughter of the house are usually the servers. For this occasion the tea is made as thick as possible and is churned with lots of fresh butter and cream. There are old stories about how the tea is judged to be thick enough and best quality for serving. After the tea is poured into the cup, a coin is set carefully over the tea. If the coin floats without sinking, then the tea is proved to be good.

Before noon every family goes to the monasteries and nunneries and temples and offers *katas* (white greeting scarves), and makes donations to the monks and nuns of food and all kinds of different gifts. A large crowd of villagers get together in the courtyard of the monastery or nunnery where the juniper and other leaves are piled. The abbot of the monastery comes out, and one of the monks starts a fire. As it burns, clouds of sweet smelling smoke will rise into the air. Now the abbot starts chanting and the rest of the monks play religious musical instruments such as drums, conchshells, large oboes, large trumpets, cymbals, and bells. The villagers all circumambulate the pile of burning incense by walking around it in a clockwise circle.

One of the monks comes out with a large plate of *tsampa* (see recipe, p 62) and passes it around to the people. Each person takes a good handful and slowly continues to walk around the pile. The abbot chants a traditional chant of victory over misfortune. Everyone joins his chanting. As they chant they raise their right hands into the air holding the *tsampa*. They will chant with the abbot three times; at the fourth, with great shouts, everyone throws the *tsampa* into the air. And it comes down like snow on everyone. Then the prayer flags are put up on tall poles, and everyone goes home and puts up their home prayer flags. Some people put them on the roofs, some on the poles in the yard.

In the afternoon, everyone starts drinking the *chang* (see recipe, p 54) that has been fermenting for the last few months. People visit each other, relatives come over. Men start playing with their *mah jong* or *sho* (a dice game) or card games. Tibetans love to gamble especially eastern Tibetans and people from Lhasa. The women dance and sing and drink *chang* too. Children play with other children and show off to each other the new sets of clothes that they have received.

Losar lasts for six or seven days. There is a lot of visiting, parties, sharing food and *chang*. The richest food, the kind not usually served, is made for this holiday. Every night there is a big fire out of doors and the boys and girls get together and have song competitions. Every night there is singing and dancing, and *Losar* is a merry time for everyone.

Even beggars who normally just get enough food to last them from day to day can get full and drunk. Once, when I was a small boy, I came across a beggar on the floor. He must have had too much to eat and drink. He told me he would give me some money if I would just roll him over to the other side of the room. I certainly tried, but he was too big for me to roll him over.

RECIPES

Note

The recipes which follow are for typical Tibetan foods and dishes. Most Tibetans learn to cook from an older person who is already a good cook, and they do not have exact, written, recipes to follow. Cooking is more a matter of experience and common sense, and getting a feel for how things go together and how they should taste and look!

Sometimes a cook in Tibet might not have one of the usual ingredients to make a dish, and all the neighbours might be out of it too. Markets are only held on certain days and variety is not great, so this can easily happen. Tibetans are used to cooking with that they have on hand. Somehow the cook will find a way round any problem, using something that is already there in the kitchen. The dish will still come out tasting good, maybe even better than usual.

If you find that you don't have an ingredient listed in one of the recipes, find a substitute that you think might work just as well. Use your own ideas and be creative. Then you will truly be cooking like a Tibetan!

Beverages

There are only a few recipes in this section, but they are important ones because of the part which beverages play in Tibetan life.

All Tibetans drink lots and lots of tea. In the recipe for making tea I have explained that some people might drink 40 cups a day. This is much more than even the British manage to consume. The traditional recipient for making tea is the sort of churn illustrated below.

A woman making tea in a churn

In Tibet, besides tea, Tibetan beer (*chang*) is the most common thing to offer to just about anyone who walks into the house. People used to drink *chang* just for special occasions, but in some parts of the country people drink *chang* more often. In the villages and towns there are no bars, but people go to the house of a family that makes *chang* and other beverages to sell, where there is often a place to sit and drink.

Monks and nuns do not drink alcoholic beverages except some followers of certain religious sects. The whole question of alcohol and Buddhism is interesting, as an examination of it in regard to *arag*, our strongest liquor, shows.

Arag is a very special beverage in Tibetan life. Not only does it please people, it even pleases the deities. It is required for certain rituals by monks and nuns. But Buddhist vows do not permit consumption of *arag* (or any alcohol) by the nuns and monks. The legend that explains why goes back to during the reign of Buddha.

Buddha had yet to disallow alcohol consumption at that time. It happened one day that one of the monks who were his followers was out begging for food. He was going from door to door. A beautiful lady, leading a goat in one hand, and carrying a large jar of *arag* in the other, was passing by. She fell in love with the monk at first sight. She approached him and asked: 'You are attractive; can you make love to me?' The monk said: 'No, I am a monk, I am not permitted.' Then the lady said: 'I am on my way to the butcher to kill this goat. Since you happen to be a man with the courage to say no to my request, can you kill this goat for me?' The monk said: 'No, I am not permitted to take lives of any kind.' Then the lady said: 'Since you refused both of my requests, can you drink some of my *arag*?'

The monk thought about it, but he didn't see any restriction imposed by the Buddha, and so he accepted the offer.

He had *arag*, and then more *arag*. Soon he was intoxicated. He then reached out to touch the lady, and made love to her; he killed the goat as well. As soon as the Buddha discovered this, he immediately outlawed the consumption of any alcohol by monks and nuns, and began to warn lay people of its dangers. Although Tibetans recognise the dangers that Buddha spoke of, they still enjoy using alcoholic beverages to liven up parties and other social occasions.

ནོད་ཇ་

BOEJA (Tibetan tea)

In Tibet, tea is made in a churn (see the drawing on p 51). After it is served, we let it sit for a while before drinking it. At least three to five cups of tea are considered necessary for everyone in the morning. And we always say a prayer of offering to the holy ones before drinking. Then we pick up the cup and carefully blow all the butter that is floating on the top of the tea to one side. If you save the butter in this way, it is good when you finish your tea to put some *tsampa* (see p 62) in the cup and mix this with it.

Most tea cups are wooden. A few times a day some one takes a little butter from the cup and lightly rubs it around the outside of the cup. This prevents the wood from cracking when the hot tea is poured in, and it gives a rich oily look. People also take the butter and rub it on their faces and behind their ears, sometimes on their hands. The cold, dry climate is very hard for the skin, and so the butter works as a skin conditioning cream.

½ cup loose Darjeeling tea
  (or Chinese fermented brick
  tea)
10 cups hot water

½ cup butter
salt to taste
1 cup heavy cream

Put the tea in the hot water and soak for 10 minutes. Then boil the tea (10 to 15 minutes for Chinese tea, 3 to 4 minutes for Darjeeling tea). Strain the tea from the pot and pour it into a churn or blender. Add the butter, salt, and cream and mix for about 3 minutes. You can mix half a quantity at a time if the blender is small. Then serve in cups.

To make tea more simply, just add salt and a lump of butter to each cup. Then pour the hot tea into this cup. This is a common way for travelers to prepare tea in Tibet.

ཆང་

CHANG (Tibetan beer)

Chang can be made from rice, wheat, corn, oats, millet and barley. If corn is used, it should be toasted and roughly ground. Some people do this for wheat, barley and oats, but it is really not necessary. These grains can be cooked whole without toasting. Although barley is most commonly used for *chang* in Tibet, rice is the quickest to ferment so we will take rice as an example.

7 cups white rice	2 tbsp brewer's yeast
water as needed	(or *pap*, p 97)
	2 tbsp sugar

Boil the rice in about 14 cups of water, just like you would for eating. Spread the cooked rice on a clean surface and let it sit until it feels cool (about 85°F: 29°C). Grind the yeast and sugar together, make it powdery. Sprinkle this yeast over the rice evenly and mix it well.

Put the rice in a barrel or in a clay jar or large glass jar, big enough to hold it all. Cover and wrap to keep it warm. We use blankets to do this, as shown in the drawing. Set the container in a warmer part of your house. Now leave it for at least 48 hours. If the cooked rice and yeast does not ferment in three days, warm the rice a bit. In Tibet we heat a rock shaped like a round ball. We make a well in the rice and put the heated rock in. Then the jar is covered and wrapped up again.

Boiled rice in pots is kept warm with blankets to help it ferment

Typical vessels for serving and drinking chang

You will know by the smell when the rice is fermented. Tibetans call this *lum,* and sometimes people just take the *lum* and fry it in a little oil. Sugar is added and it is eaten as a treat.

To make *chang,* put the *lum* in a bigger jar or leave it in the same one if it will hold 15 cups of water on top and has a tight cover. Add 15 cups of cold water. Stir this and put the cover on. Make it airtight. Now set it in a cool place for ageing. *Chang* made with rice should age at least 2 weeks before drinking, but it is better to leave it longer. Other grains must be left for longer. Some could age at least 3 to 6 months. In Tibet the jar is sealed with mud and sometimes with yak-dung or beeswax. In the UK or USA a refrigerator can be used.

Strain off the *chang* (liquor) and serve it. Put the *lum* back into the container. Then add less water and age for a longer time than you did at first. You can add water and drain off the *chang* up to three times. But after that it will not be good any more. In Tibet the exhausted *lum* is fed to livestock.

In Tibet, we serve *chang* from containers of the kinds shown in the drawing, pouring it into cups or glasses.

You can drink *chang* cold or you can warm it up. If you warm it, add a little sugar, then drink it.

NOTE. For barley *chang,* use brewer's barley.

རྡོང་པ (ཤིང་ཆང་)

DONGPA (SHING CHANG) (Tibetan hot toddy)

In Tibet we have a specially made container of wood for drinking *dongpa*. It is called *dongpa* when empty and *shing chang* when full, and it looks like a little barrel. The hollow tube is made from cane or bamboo and the holes at the bottom are made in the side of the tube instead of in the end. The holes are covered with a wrapping of thread so only the liquid comes through, and not the grains.

The drawing shows the hot toddy, with grains foaming up at the top, in its Tibetan container.

   Dongpa is always made from millet, very seldom from wheat or oats.

6 cups millet
4 tsp brewer's yeast or *pap* (see p 97)
3 tsp sugar

Cook the millet just like rice — boil in about 12 cups of water until water is absorbed — and spread it over a clean surface. Let it sit until it is cool to the touch, but not cold. Sprinkle the yeast over the millet and gently mix it well. Put the mixture into a barrel or large jar that has a cover. Cover it and wrap in blankets. Let it ferment in a warmer part of your house. The temperature should be around 70° to 80°F (21°-26°C). It will take 4 to 5 days before it ferments sufficiently. Then open it and sprinkle a little cold water on the fermented millet, just enough to make it moist. Put all the grain and the liquid into a container and make it airtight. Set it in a cool place to age. (In Tibet we put it in a basement or unheated room for several months. In the UK or USA it can be left in the refrigerator). It must age at least 2-3 weeks.

Fill a large glass to about ¾ full with mash (fermented grain and liquid). Pour boiling water over it, stir, and allow it to sit for a few minutes. Then serve. It should be drunk through a narrow hollow tube like bamboo or a straw, so that you only take the liquid and not the kernels of millet in the bottom. Keep adding hot water as you drink until the flavor is weak.

ཨ་རག

ARAG (Distilled liquor)   serves 2-3

The recipe requires only one ingredient, apart from water. You must have some *chang* (see recipe on p 54).

The utensil is the most important thing. You can use a steamer with several stacking layers. The lowest layer has a solid, unperforated bottom, and the upper layers have perforated bottoms to allow the steam to rise through them. You also need a cover that is deeply curved or pointed at the center. This will be turned upside down to cover the top layer fully and thus keep the steam inside. The curved or pointed shape is necessary so that condensed drops will collect at the center and drip into the bowl below (see illustration). A wok with the top layer set upright will also work for this purpose.

Add water to the *chang* mash to make it slushy. The mixture should be about the consistency of a watery pea soup. Pour it into the bottom (unperforated) layer of the steamer (1). Set the second (perforated) layer of the steamer (2) on top of this. Place your smaller bowl (3) in the center of this upper part of the steamer. Put the cover on upside down (4) and fill it up with cold water.

Now bring the *chang* to a boil over a high heat. Then, once you start to hear it boiling, lower the heat. In the meantime, it is very important to keep changing the water in the top vessel (lid or wok) as it gets hot, and replace it with cold water. If you add ice cubes, the water won't have to be changed as often. Steam it for anywhere from 15 to 25 minutes, depending on how much *chang* you have boiling. Be sure no steam is leaking out. You can use wet, clean rags to cover the gaps around the lid.

Now remove the cover gently, and you will find the smaller container inside the steamer has your *arag* in it.

Non-Meat Dishes

Cereals are a main feature of the Tibetan diet, and the first recipes in this section are all for staple cereal dishes. Being able to make *tsampa* is very important for anyone wanting to eat in truly Tibetan style. But many of the recipes are easy to make with commonly available vegetables and other simple ingredients.

A bowl of tsampa

DRESIL (sweet rice)   serves 3-4

In Tibet *dresil* is served as a special offering for New Year's day, a wedding, or another special occasion. Tibetans use a lot more butter, at least twice as much as Americans would, because the climate is cold and dry. In Tibet there are no health problems from always eating a lot of fat.

4 cups long grain white rice	½ cup whole cashew nuts
water for cooking the rice	½ cup raisins
½ cup melted butter	½ cup brown sugar

Boil the rice just like you normally would. It is better if it is a little dry and fluffy. In Tibet the rice is cooked until it is half done, then put in a steamer and steamed until finished. This way it is fluffy, not sticky.

Add the butter and mix it well. Then add the nuts and raisins and sugar. Mix them in well but very gently. Serve with a bowl of yoghurt on the side.

NOTES. In Tibet we also add *droma*, a small very sweet root vegetable something like a tiny sweet potato. We have not found this here in the USA. Our raisins and nuts mostly come from India.

ཡོས་

YOE (Toasted grain)

In Tibet people eat *yoe* as snacks or as lunch while travelling or herding animals.

1 lb of either barley, wheat, corn, millet or soybeans

Wash the grain and then soak it in the water for 10 minutes (except soybeans). Then drain and spread the grain thinly on a piece of cloth or clean surface to dry in the sun. Leave for 45 to 60 minutes or until dry.

Roast about a pound of grain at a time in a heavy cast-iron pan over medium heat. Stir it continuously until the grain is a nice brown and partly popped.

This popped or toasted grain is called *yoe*. Barley or wheat *yoe* is nice to eat all by itself. Maize *yoe* is popcorn if it pops, which it may not. You can also toast the kernels of slightly green corn. They are chewy and very good; but, of course they do not pop. Alternatively, *yoe* can be made with young snow peas.

ཙམ་པ་

TSAMPA (Tibetan toasted flour)

Tsampa is the main staple of Tibet. It is usually made from barley, but it can also be made from wheat, corn, millet, oats, even soybeans. *Tsampa* just means flour made from toasted grain. Of course the most common *tsampa* in Tibet is made from barley, and that is what people think of when they hear the word *tsampa*.

4 lb toasted barley or *yoe* (you can use any of the grains mentioned in the *yoe* recipe on the preceding page)

Grind the toasted grain in a flour mill* until it is as fine as flour. Now it is *tsampa*. *Tsampa* can be eaten in many different ways. You can just add cold water, stir it up and drink; or you can add tea to *tsampa* and drink it. You can also just pick up a handful and chew it up. It is also used for cooking and many other things.

The preparation of *tsampa* is usually the same all over Tibet. Sometimes people will heat up fine sand in a large, heavy pan. Then the grain is poured into the heated sand and stirred. This way it toasts evenly and does not burn. There is a special little broom made for stirring *yoe* as it toasts. After toasting, the sand and grain are poured into a sifter and the sand is strained out.

*   In Tibet, each house usually has a quern, a stone mill, for grinding that is turned by hand. But large amounts of *yoe* (grain) are taken to the miller. Amost every large village has a mill. The heavy stone millstones are turned by a waterwheel like the one used as shown on p 27. The water is carried from a nearby stream by a chute and rushes down over the waterwheel to make it turn.

ཚམ་ཐུག

TSAMTUK (Tsampa soup)   serves 3-4

2 cups *tsampa** (see p 62)   1 cup toasted soybeans
7 cups water   1 cup any hard grated cheese
½ stick (2 oz/60g) butter   or *chura* (see p 96)
   or margarine   salt to taste

Add the *tsampa* to the water while cold and stir well. Bring to a boil. Add the butter and the toasted soybeans. (If the soybeans are still raw, you can toast them by spreading them in a single layer in the bottom of a dry frying pan and stirring or shaking the pan continuously over medium heat, until the kernels split). Simmer for 5 minutes. Add salt to taste. Now you can add the cheese and serve in bowls. (if you are using *chura*, you should add it with the soybeans, not right before serving.)

* Instead of *tsampa* you can substitute cornmeal.

 སྦག་

PAG (Tsampa cake)   serves 3-4

6 cups *tsampa* (see p 62)   1 cup ground cheese
2 cups hot tea   (or *chur ship*, see p 96)
½ cup melted butter   ½ cup brown sugar

Add butter, cheese, and sugar to the hot tea and stir. Put the *tsampa* in
and mix and knead it well with your hands, to make a stiff dough.
Shape this into a flat square about one inch thick. Cut into pieces just
like a cake and serve.

This is a very common food of the monks and nuns in Tibet. Each
person mixes his own *pag* in a bowl or cup, but it takes some practice.
This is how it is done. When people are served tea, they blow the
butter that floats on top to one side and drink the tea. Then when
there is just a little tea and the butter left, they add some *tsampa*. The
tsampa is mixed in with one hand rubbing the flour, tea, and butter
against the inside of the cup, while the other hand holds the cup and
turns it in the opposite direction. When everything is mixed into a
stiff dough, the *pag* can be rolled into little balls and popped into the
mouth. Things can be added to make the *pag* fancy, but basic *pag* is
just butter, tea, *tsampa* and sugar.

Sometimes travellers carry a small leather bag called *pulkhug* or
thangug. To prepare *pag* they put all the ingredients in this bag, tie up
the mouth, and then rub it gently as they are walking along. This way
they can mix their *pag* without stopping. But there is a secret to
making *pag* in this way. The *tsampa* must go into the bag first. If the tea
and butter go in first, the bag will get wet and everything will stick to
it. Then you will have a mess, not *pag*.

SENGONG (Sherpa-style *tsampa* cake)

Sherpa means easterner and it is a name for Tibetans who originally migrated from Eastern Tibet, and who now live in the foothills of the Himalayas, by the border with Nepal. The Nepalese use the word too, but for them it is just a name and does not mean easterner. My mother is a Sherpa, but my father came from another part of Tibet and he was not a Sherpa. So I am half a Sherpa.

As for this Sherpa-style cake, Tibetans never chew it — they just swallow the chunks whole. *Sengong* is mostly eaten in the southern parts of the country and it is a very important food in the Himalayas.

6 cups *tsampa*, or millet flour*	4 cups water
½ tbsp salt	½ cup butter

Use a round-bottomed pan or wok if available. Add the salt to the water and bring to a boil. Add all the *tsampa* or flour. Stir and turn with a hard wooden spatula. Keep stirring and turning over a high heat until it forms a thick dough. Lower the heat and keep stirring and turning for another 3 minutes. Remove from heat. Now take four round dinner plates and put some butter or hot tomato sauce (see *pagma* recipe, p 76) on each. Put one quarter of the *sengong* dough on each plate. It will make a thick patty. Then flop the dough over on the plate so the top is smooth and coated with the butter or sauce.

Press a well in the center of the dough and put a pat of butter in. Serve *sengong* with hot tomato sauce (*pagma*) on the same plate. This is usually eaten with the hands by pulling off a lump at a time and rolling it in the sauce.

* If we use other flours instead of *tsampa*, they take longer to cook.

ཀྲི་མོག་མོག་

TRIMOMO (Steamed bread)   serves 2-3

2 cups whole wheat flour   1 tsp baking yeast
2 cups white flour   1 tsp baking soda
lukewarm water as needed   1 cup oil
                                                   2 tsp turmeric

Add yeast and baking soda to 1 cup of lukewarm water. Stir until all the yeast is dissolved. Combine the two flours. Add 1 cup of the mixed flour to the water. Stir it well. Let it sit 2 — 3 hours in a warm place. Add the rest of the flour and knead a dough. Add water if necessary. The dough should be stiff but not too stiff. Break the dough into two halves. Roll it out until it is about ⅛ inch thin. Mix the oil and turmeric together. Apply a thin, even coat of this to the surface of the dough (as shown in fig.1).

Roll the flattened dough into a log (fig. 2). It will be about 3 inches in diameter. Slice the log up into 2 inch pieces (fig.3), and shape each of these in turn into a *trimomo*. The way you do it is to take each section and hold it upright with your thumbs in front and fingers behind, then squeeze with your thumbs until the middle part becomes much thinner (fig. 4). As you do this, the thicker top and bottom will bend round your thumbs, towards you, and will eventually meet.

The next step is to put the piece of dough down on a flat surface, thick part underneath and thin part uppermost. Then insert your forefingers into it, one from each side. Keeping them in this position, grasp the dough between your thumbs (in front) and second fingers (behind), then twist the whole thing (fig. 5) by turning your right hand 90° away from you and your left hand 90° towards you. This will make the ends open into a flower shape and bring the sides together at the bottom (fig. 6). Round this bottom part and flatten it so that the *trimomo* can sit in the steamer.

ALTERNATIVE METHOD OF SHAPING. You can also just pull the dough off in chunks and roll each chunk into a ball about 1½ inches in diameter. Flatten the bottom and sides, leaving the top rounded. Cut a cross on the top with a knife (just a slight cut, not all the way).

Apply a thin coat of butter or margarine to the steamer. Put the *trimomo* in it, in rows, with a little space between them so that they do not touch each other. Steam for 15 to 20 minutes over a high heat.

The *trimomo*, which look like flowers if made the first way, are usually eaten with curry or some other sauces.

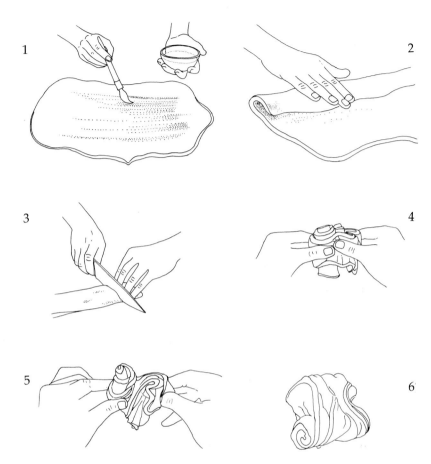

ཁ་ཟས་

KAPSE (Fried bread)

3 cups whole wheat flour
3 cups white flour
3 tsp baking powder*
3 cups nonfat milk

4 tsp brown sugar
1½ quarts (3 pints) oil
    for deep frying

Combine the flours and the baking powder. Mix the milk and sugar in another bowl until the sugar is all dissolved. Add the milk to the flours and mix to knead a dough. The dough should be stiffer than bread dough. Tear the dough off into half cup size pieces. Make these into balls and roll them out flat. (*Kapse* can be shaped in many different ways, but this one is easiest for me to describe.)

In a deep skillet heat the oil until it is very hot. Fry one bread at a time until lightly browned. You can eat the *kapse* plain or along with yoghurt or curry, even with something sweet like honey.

* In Tibet baking powder comes from the area where natural salt is found; it is called *pueto*. Some people like to make breads using yeasts so they do not have the taste of the baking powder. To make yeast add almost anything sour, such as vinegar, to milk and then allow the mixture to sit for a while. (See the yeast recipe, p 97.)

བག་ཚ་མར་ཁུ་

BAKTSA MARKU (Sweet dumplings)   serves 2-3

1 cup whole wheat flour	½ cup butter
2 cups white flour	¼ cup sugar (brown)*
water as needed (& salt)	½ cup ground cheese (*chura*)

Combine the flours and add water to make a stiff dough. Cut the dough into four equal pieces and roll these into a snake-like shape, about the thickness of your little finger. Cut these into half inch pieces. You can sprinkle some flour over the dumplings to prevent them from sticking together.

Boil about 3 quarts (6 pints) of water, sprinkle 1 teaspoon of salt in the water. Add all the dumplings and boil them for 10 minutes. Drain. Heat the butter in a round-bottomed pan or large skillet. Add brown sugar and stir. Add the dumplings and stir gently while cooking. Sprinkle the ground cheese over the dumplings and serve.

* The raw brown sugar is imported to Tibet from Nepal and India. The sugar cane is squeezed and the juice is boiled for a long period of time. Then the juice sits in a cool place until it hardens. After that it is sliced into smaller pieces and used for brown sugar.

DRAWOE KURA (Tibetan buckwheat pancake)   serves 2-3

4 cups sifted buckwheat flour
1 cup buttermilk or *dara*

Add buttermilk to the flour and beat well, add some water if needed.
You should have runny batter just like pancake batter. The griddle*
should be quite hot when you first pour the batter on so it won't stick.
But then the heat should be lowered as the bread cooks so it won't
burn. Pour a half cup of the batter on to the center of the griddle. Flop
it over when the cake is cooked on one side. Serve with a cup of plain
yoghurt and honey if you have some.†

* In Tibet griddles are mostly metal, but sometimes they are made of
clay or even just a thin flat piece of stone.

† Yoghurt is a very common food, but honey is unusual and would
be used on special occasions. *Buram* or brown sugar is used to
sweeten food.

ཡ་སྱོ་

YABA (Buckwheat green salad)   serves 2-3

2 bunches young green
    buckwheat leaves* or
    1 bunch spinach and
    1 bunch watercress
1 tsp honey
2 cloves crushed garlic

½ tsp red pepper
salt to taste
1 cup yoghurt (plain)
1 tbsp oil
¼ tsp fenugreek seeds

Wash the greens thoroughly, having cut the stems off; then drain the water. Coarsely chop the greens and put them in a salad bowl. Now put the honey, garlic, red pepper and salt in a small cup and add ¼ cup of hot water. Stir and mix well, and pour over the salad. (Make sure the honey is dissolved well). Add all the yoghurt over the greens and mix well gently. Now heat the oil and brown the fenugreek seeds and pour over the green salad.

*   The buckwheat green is not common here in the States. I therefore tried spinach and watercress together, and this combination brings the closest flavor to the buckwheat green. But in Tibet, we do not have watercress, and spinach is not common in many parts of the country.

ཞོགས་ཁོག་ཁ་ཚ་

SHOGOK KATSA (Hot potato curry)   serves 4-5

4 lb potatoes
½ cup chopped tomatoes
1 tsp hot chili
2 cloves of crushed garlic
½ tsp grated ginger
¼ tsp turmeric
salt to taste

1 medium size shallot,
   chopped
2 tbsp olive or vegetable oil
½ tsp fenugreek seeds
½ cup thinly sliced bell
   pepper

Boil the potatoes until they are cooked, then peel and dice them. In a blender, put everything except potatoes, oil, fenugreek, and sliced bell pepper. Blend until everything is mashed. Heat the oil and brown the fenugreek seeds, then add the mixture from the blender. Stir well and cook over high heat for 1 minute. Pour the mixture over the potatoes and mix gently until well mixed. Then garnish with the slices of bell pepper.

ཞོགས་ཁོག་གོབ་བཙོས་

SHOGOK GOPTSE (Tibetan style potato curry)   serves 3-4

In many parts of Tibet most vegetables do not grow. For instance, where the nomads live practically nothing grows but grass because of the high altitude. Therefore the nomads use mostly meat as food. But there has always been trading between the nomads and farmers. The farmers in the warmer valleys dry the vegetables that they grow such as mushrooms, radishes, turnips, potatoes and many others. Then they trade with the nomads for the produce the nomads have — butter, cheese, meat, fat and wool. The nomads usually come to trade in the summer, and their main needs are non-animal products. So a dish like *shogok goptse* would be a very special treat for them.

2 lb potatoes, peeled and thinly
    sliced*
1 cup chopped tomatoes
½ cup thinly sliced green onion
1 cup sliced bell pepper
½ cup finely chopped white
    onion
4 tsp oil

½ tsp fenugreek
¼ cup soy sauce
½ tsp minced ginger
½ tsp turmeric powder
½ tsp cumin powder
2 cloves crushed garlic
salt to taste

Heat the oil in a wok or skillet big enough to hold all the ingredients. Put the fenugreek seeds in and stir over medium heat until they are dark brown. Add the garlic and chopped white onion. Stir until lightly browned. Add the tomatoes and all spices. Stir well. Cover and cook over low heat for 3 minutes or so.

Add the potatoes and 1 cup of water. Stir, then cook for 10 minutes or until the potatoes are tender. Add the sliced bell pepper and stir gently. Cook for 2 minutes longer.

Take off from the heat and sprinkle the chopped green onion over the potatoes, and then do not stir again until ready to serve. This is good with rice, bread, *sengong*, *pag*, etc.

*   You can substitute any kind of vegetable for potatoes to make it as curry.

ལ་སྐྱུར་ (ཚོས་ན་ལ་ཕུག་)

LAKYUR (SOEN LAFUG)(Pickled radishes or cabbages)

2 medium size daikon radishes
   or 1 small cabbage
½ cup vinegar
5 cloves sliced garlic
2 tsp hot pepper

½ tsp szechuan pepper
   or black pepper
2 cups water
½ tsp caraway seeds

Get a large glass or clay jar with a tight cover. It should be big enough to hold all the ingredients. Slice the radishes or cabbage thinly and put the slices in the jar. Then pour the vinegar and water over them and add the other ingredients. Mix well, cover the jar and make it airtight. Leave it in the direct sun or somewhere warm (80°–90°F; 26°-32°C). You have to wait 10 to 15 days before opening the jar. Serve as a side dish for rice, *momo* (p 82), or other things. If you like you may sprinkle with salt on the plate (not in the jar). These pickles are also good with *chang* and beer.

ཤ་མོ་བསྲེག

SHAM TRAK (Baked mushroom)   serves 2-3

Shamo is the Tibetan name for mushrooms. There are many kinds of mushrooms in Tibet, which are prepared in various ways. These include a red one which grows on trees and is *taak* (blood) *shamo*. But the one most commonly found in American and European markets is often prepared this way.

1 lb large mushrooms
½ stick (2 oz/60 g) butter
salt to taste

Remove all the stems. Then clean the outside of each mushroom by using a clean damp cloth or paper towel. Put all the mushrooms on greaseproof paper or baking tin facing down. Now bake them in the oven at 350°-400°F (175°-205°C) for 2 minutes. Take them out and put bits of butter in each mushroom where the stem used to be. Sprinkle with a little salt to taste. Bake in oven again for 3 more minutes. Then serve as a side dish or snack.

པག་མ་

PAGMA (Hot tomato sauce)

2 cups chopped tomatoes*
3 tsp olive oil or vegetable oil
½ tsp fenugreek seeds
3 cloves crushed garlic

½ cup finely chopped white
    onion
3 tsp red chili pepper
2 tsp soy sauce
salt to taste
1 cup water

Heat the oil in a skillet. Add the fenugreek seeds and stir until they are dark brown. Add the chopped garlic and onion and stir until they are lightly browned. Now add the tomatoes, red pepper, soy sauce, and salt. Stir well and cook gently over low heat for 8 to 10 minutes. Add water and keep stirring until the tomatoes are mushy. Add salt to taste. Serve as a side dish with something like *sengong*, rice, *momo*, breads, *trimomo*, etc.

* Tomatoes are not usually found in Tibet, except in the southern part. Instead of tomatoes we use something called *shosha* or *churul*. This is a kind of cheese made from cream and skin of the milk. It is very tasty when you get used to it. Limburger can be tried as a substitute for *churul* or *shosha*; and any soft strong-flavored cheese will also work.

Meat Dishes

Chapter 10 explains the attitude of Tibetans to eating meat. Although they are Buddhists, this attitude permits the consumption of meat and we have many meat recipes. But there are no widespread recipes for fish or wild birds. Fish are scarce in many areas; and generally people prefer to eat the meat of larger creatures, since fewer need to be butchered to provide enough meat.

Sheep's head, traditionally a feature of the Tibetan New Year's Day. See recipe for Luggo *(page 88)*

 རུས་ཐང་

RUETANG (Broth soup)   serves 3-4

In Tibet no part of a butchered animal is wasted. The bones can be kept for a long time in the meat storage room of the house where they stay cold and dry because of the climate. Before the bones are used they are smashed into small chunks with a pestle in a big mortar that is usually kept outside the house. This is called a *tsom*.

3lb marrow bones   ½ cup finely chopped cilantro
3 tsp salt (or to taste)   (coriander)
4 beaten eggs   15 cups water

Put the bones in water and bring to a boil. Simmer on a low heat uncovered for 30 to 40 minutes. If the bones you use are not in small pieces, you may want to cook them longer, even for several hours, to extract more flavor. When you do this, keep the cover on at least part of the time to keep the broth from cooking away. Drain the broth from the bones. Then add the beaten eggs and the salt. Blend or mix well. Add the cilantro, stir, and serve in bowls.

*Breaking up bones
in a* tsom *or mortar*

ནས་ཐུག

SATUK (Nettle soup)   serves 2-3

Milaraspa, Tibet's world famous poet and saint, lived solely on this soup for many years, until he turned green. Above Kyirong Valley or Happy Valley in Tibet is one of Mila's famous meditation caves. The surroundings are completely barren, except for a long strip of nettles which starts at the cave and goes all the way to the valley. People say that Mila accidentally dropped his soup pot one day, and that this strip marks its path as it rolled downhill.

1lb nettle leaves (approximately)	salt to taste
	½ tsp crushed ginger
6 cups meat broth of any kind	1 tbsp flour for thickening
½ tsp Szechuan or black pepper	½ cup milk

When you go out to pick the nettle greens, be sure to wear a pair of gloves and use a pair of scissors to cut them. And cut only the top young greens from the plants less than 1ft high, not the lower and older leaves. (Nettle leaves are easily dried and stored. If dry leaves are used reduce the quantity in the recipe.)

Wash the leaves thoroughly, but again do not use bare hands. Cut away the unnecessary stems and use only the green leaves. Boil the broth and add the nettle greens. Add also the Szechuan or black pepper, the salt and the ginger. Simmer for at least 30 to 40 minutes or until the greens are completely done and puree them. Now add the flour and milk. Mix and beat with a wire whisk to make sure the greens are pureed. Serve with rice or any other dish as a soup.

བོད་ཐུག

BOETUK (Dumpling soup)   serves 5-6

3 cups whole wheat flour
3 cups white flour
water as needed
3 lb marrow bones or joints
   or just soup bones
2 tbsp oil
½ tsp fenugreek seeds
½ cup sliced onion
½ cup chopped green onion
1 tsp minced garlic

1 cup chopped tomatoes
1 tsp minced ginger
½ tsp grated nutmeg
¼ tsp turmeric
1 lb lean beef or lamb
salt to taste
3 tsp soy sauce
2 cups sliced radishes
1 cup green peas

Combine the flours and add water to make a stiff dough. Roll between your hands into a long snake shape the thickness of your little finger. Cut into half inch pieces, which are the dumplings. You can sprinkle some flour lightly over the dumplings to keep them from sticking together.

Boil about 15 cups of water, add the bones, and simmer for 20 to 30 minutes. In another pot heat the oil. Add the fenugreek seeds and stir until dark brown. Add the garlic and sliced onion and stir until lightly browned. Add tomatoes and all the spices. Stir gently, cover and cook for 1 minute over medium heat. Then add the meat, salt, and also soy sauce. Stir and mix together. Cover and cook for 15 minutes or until the meat is tender. Add a little water if necessary. Add the sliced radishes and peas and stir. Cook for 2 more minutes.

Now strain the broth into the other ingredients and bring to a boil. Add the dumplings and boil for 6 to 8 minutes or until the dumplings are done. Finally, add the chopped green onions. Then the soup will be ready to serve. It is usually served in bowls with hot sauce as a side dish.

NOTE. You can substitute egg noodles for the dumplings.

ༀབག་ལེབ་

SHAPALÉ (Meat pastry)   serves 4-5

2 lb lean ground beef
    or lamb*
½ cup hot water
2 cups finely chopped celery
    or green onion
½ cup minced white onion
salt to taste
1 tsp ground cumin
½ tsp grated nutmeg
1 tsp fresh ground ginger

3 cups whole wheat flour
3 cups white flour
1 tsp baking powder
cold water as needed

Add the hot water, celery, onions, salt and all the spices to the ground meat and mix well. Set aside. Combine the two flours and baking soda. Add water and mix well to knead a stiff dough. Break off about a half cup piece at a time. Roll it out so it is flat and round, just like a tortilla. Put a half cup of the meat mixture in the middle of the dough circle and flatten it down a little. Then put another dough circle on the top. Now pinch tightly all around the edge to stick the two circles together. Continue the same process with the remaining dough and mixture. Bake the pastry circles in a 300°-350°F (150°-175°C) oven for 40 to 60 minutes or until their surface is lightly browned.

If you want to deep fry in oil, the filling has to be lightly fried in 3 teaspoons of oil for at least 5 minutes before filling the pastry. Then heat about 5 cups of oil in a pan. The oil should be shallow enough so it does not cover the seam of the meat pastry. Brown one side first. Then turn and brown the other side.

*   Instead of meat you can substitute spinach, mushrooms, cauliflower, fresh radish leaves, mustard greens, green peas, and other things with your desired spices. All the vegetables have to be fried in 3 teaspoons of oil along with the spices before they are put in the pastry.

ཚོག་མོག

MOMO (Steamed meat-filled dumplings)   serves 4-5

Momo (the same word is used for both the singular and plural) are a very special treat in Tibet. Their importance in the eyes of Tibetans has even made them the subject of a proverb. If someone is a scold or talks too much, Tibetans say: KHA MOMO NANGSHIN DHE (last word pronounced 'day') 'Keep your mouth like a momo (i e closed)'. At a formal meal or a celebration, one of the dishes will be *momo*. People fold them up in different shapes to fit the occasions; some are simple like the ones in this recipe and some are very fancy. Some are made with a tiny hole left in the top so the juice can be sucked out before the *momo* is eaten.

Tibetans learn how to make *momo* from the time they are very young. In Tibet a cook starts out to make *momo* for many people with a big pile of dough on one side and a big pile of meat filling on the other. A good cook uses the last bit of dough for the last bit of filling and has nothing left over.

Any flat steamer such as a Japanese steamer can be used to make *momo*. If nothing is available, you can even bake them in an oven or boil them.

The sort of steamer which Tibetans use for making *momo*, and for steaming other things too, is shown in the drawing.

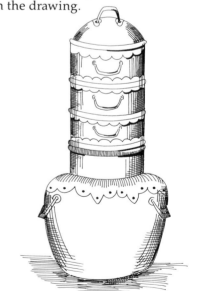

2 lb lean ground beef
   or lamb
⅓ cup hot water
1 cup finely chopped celery
½ cup finely chopped green
   onion
salt to taste
½ tsp ground cumin
½ tsp grated nutmeg
½ tsp freshly ground ginger

and for the dough
3 cups white flour
3 cups well sifted whole
   wheat flour
water as needed
1 tsp baking soda

Add hot water, celery, onion, salt and all the spices to the ground meat. Mix well and set aside.

Combine the flours with the baking soda. Add water and mix well to make a stiff dough. Pull off a small chunk of dough, about an inch or ping pong ball size and roll it into a ball. Flatten it slightly with your hands and dust both sides with flour. Roll over the flattened ball once with a rolling pin. Then roll the dough flat using the roller from the edge of the dough into the middle. Push the roller over the dough with your right hand and turn the dough a little with your left hand after each roll. When you have rolled all around the dough you will have a flat circle about 4 inches across that is just a little thicker in the middle — just as it should be to hold the stuffing.

You can alternatively roll a larger quantity of dough out with a rolling pin and cut small circles with a cookie cutter; in that case, you will have to pinch the edges of each circle thinner by hand.

The easiest way to stuff a *momo* is this. Put a teaspoon of the meat mixture on your dough circle. Fold the circle in half. Now you will have a flat half-moon shape (see fig. 1). Pinch the edges together. Really pinch, do not be gentle here because you have to seal the edges together so the juices do not leak out while steaming. Bend the *momo* along the straight side (fig. 2) and pinch once more on the edge right above the bend to reseal it at the bend. The *momo* will now have assumed the shape shown in fig. 3 and can sit up in the steamer (fig. 4). Continue to make *momo* until you use up all the dough and filling.

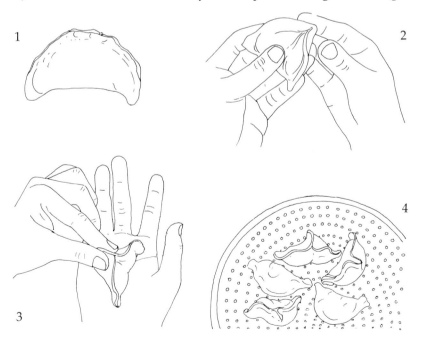

ALTERNATIVE FOLDING. A different traditional way of folding a *momo* starts with the same dough circle. The dough is placed on the palm and fingers of your left hand. The fingers are slightly spread. Put a spoonful of meat mixture in the middle. Now take a little pinch of dough at the edge, pinch hard. Take another pinch about a fingertip away and pinch this so that it sticks to the first tuck you did. Turn the dough a little with your left hand and pinch again. Again stick the new pinch to the old ones. As you turn, use the thumb of your left hand to keep the filling in place. (The secret is to never touch the filling with your right hand. If you do it will get too sticky to fold the dough.) Take your pinches from the edges of the dough which you fold on top of the meat, not to the side. The most important secret is to pinch hard so the edges stick together well. Keep going around the circle, pinching with one hand, poking the meat in with the other until you reach the end. If there is a hole, just pinch your last tuck to your first.

Now get ready for steaming. Rub and coat the steamer with butter or margarine. Put each *momo* in the steamer as you finish it and make sure the *momo* are not touching each other or the sides of the steamer, or they will stick together when they are done. Boil the water (about 5 to 8 cups depending on the size of the steamer) in the bottom part of the steamer set. It must be a full boil. Then put on the upper part of the steamer, containing the *momo*, with a tight lid and steam for 10 to 12 minutes. Serve while hot, usually with a hot sauce (see pp 91-2), and soy sauce, and *ruetang* (see p 78). Cold beer goes well with this dish.

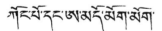

KONGPOE or AMDOE MOMO

Use the same ingredients as for *momo* but substitute ground pork for beef or lamb. Brown the pork in a frying pan, breaking it into small bits for stuffing the *momo*. Then prepare *momo* as in the previous recipe.

Kongpo and Amdo are famous as the parts of Tibet where people raise pigs and eat pork. Their pork versions of traditional Tibetan meat dishes are a special regional style of Tibetan cooking. By using pork you can make Kongpo/Amdo style versions of other meat dishes, such as *shapalé* (p 81), *shabril* (p 85), or soups that include meat.

ཤ་སྦྲིལ་

SHABRIL (Meatball curry)   serves 3-4

2 lb lean ground beef
 or lamb
4 tsp oil
¼ tsp fenugreek seeds
½ cup chopped onion
½ tsp crushed ginger
2 cloves crushed garlic
¼ tsp turmeric
salt to taste
2 tsp soy sauce

2 cups thinly sliced mushrooms*
 (save the stems)
1 cup thinly sliced radishes
1 cup sour cream†
½ cup thinly chopped green
 onion

Make the meat into half inch balls. Heat the oil in a round bottomed pan or any deep skillet. Add the fenugreek seeds and stir until they are dark brown. Add the onion and stir until it is slightly browned. Add the meatballs and stir very gently. Add all the spices and the salt and the soy sauce, cover and cook over low heat for 5 minutes. Blend the mushroom stems with one cup of water and pour over the meat. Add sliced mushrooms and radishes, stir and cook for 10 minutes more or until the radishes are tender.

Remove from heat and add sour cream. Stir gently but well. Then sprinkle the green onion over the top. Do not stir at all. This can be served with rice or breads.

* In Tibet there are many different kinds of mushrooms. People collect them during the summer when the rains fall and dry them to save for the other seasons. It is all right to use ordinary mushrooms in this dish.

† For sour cream we use the cream that floats on heated milk. The richest milk comes from the *dzomo*. The *dzo* and *dzomos* are a crossbreed of a male yak with female cow.

ཤ་སྐམ་པོ་

SHA KAMPO (Dried meat)

In Tibet it does not rain very much and the air is very dry due to the high altitude. People can dry whole carcasses and sides of meat in the sun. Most houses also have a special room for making *sha kampo* and storing meat. In the winter the meat is cut into strips and put over rods in this room. The strips can be very thick, for in the Tibetan climate the water in the meat soon freezes into large crystals. Then these evaporate too and the meat becomes very dry like cork or soft wood. Meat that has been dried this way is very tender to eat uncooked or cooked and is very good.

5lb lean beef or lamb
4 tsp salt
3 cups lukewarm water

Cut the meat into strips about ½ inch thick and 4 to 5 inches long. Put the salt in the lukewarm water and dip each strip into the water. Hang the strips of meat in rows on a string either over your stove or out in the sun. Make some kind of covering to keep the flies away. The strips should hang for 2 to 3 days, and the meat will reduce to around 2 pounds. It can be stored for a long time if kept dry. This dried meat can be eaten as a snack by itself or it can substitute for meat of any kind in cooking.

LOWA (Stuffed lung)   serves 2-3

Since most Tibetans are Buddhist they do not like to take lives of other beings just to eat. This is specially true in the lands where farmers grow grains and vegetables and rarely eat meat. The only times they do eat meat is when an animal is killed by other beasts or falls from a cliff. If they do find meat like this, it is considered a great luxury. They eat the meat because the animal is already dead anyway. Even so, they use every part of the body and nothing is wasted. There are ways of using all the different parts of an animal, such as the lungs in this recipe; and even the hooves are used as toys for the children.

1 complete sheep or goat's lung with windpipe still on	2 tsp finely ground cumin
4 egg yolks	¼ tsp turmeric powder
1 cup well-sifted white flour	½ tsp finely ground nutmeg
water as needed	4 tsp oil
2 cloves well crushed garlic	salt to taste

Wash the lung in lukewarm water and squeeze it out gently. Let all the juice run out by holding it upside down. Blow the lung up by breathing into the windpipe.* Close the windpipe so the air cannot get out and dip the lung in water to see if it is airtight. (If it leaks, it cannot be used.) Set the lung aside.

Put the flour, egg yolks and all the spices in a bowl. Add about 2-3 cups of water and mix and beat well. This will make a very runny batter. Gently fill the lung through the windpipe with the batter by using a funnel or a pastry bag with the pipe on. (A pastry bag of the sort used by bakers for decorating large cakes can be used.) When the filling reaches up into the windpipe, blow it down again and keep pouring in more batter until the lung is completely filled up. Bend the windpipe back and tie it with a strong string. Boil the lung in at least 2 gallons of water or enough water and space so the lung floats around while it is boiling. Cook for 20 to 25 minutes.

When done, drain and let the lung cool. Slice it just like a bread. Heat the oil in a skillet and fry the slices on both sides until nice and slightly browned. Sprinkle with salt to your taste.

*   The traditional way to blow the lung up is by mouth; but someone asked me if you could not use a bicycle pump or take it down to your local gas station instead. I have never tried these methods myself.

ལུག་མགོ།

LUGGO (Sheep's head)   serves 2-3

In Tibet this is one of the most important dishes to be served on Losar, New Year's Day. The tradition originated during the reign of the *Bon* religion before Buddhism came to the country. In those days the *Bon* religion included many sacrificial rites. The sheep's head was put on the altar after they sacrificed the sheep on New Year's Day as part of the offering.

After Buddhism came to Tibet, the *Bon* religion nearly vanished. However, some of its traditions blended with Tibetan Buddhism. Tibetan Buddhists never sacrifice animals for religious offerings; but it is significant that we still make a sheep's head out of *tsampa* dough and put it on the altar as a traditional offering for New Year.

When we serve sheep's head, we sometimes save the juices from the meat. We leave the juice overnight in a cooler part of the room. The next day, it turns into a kind of aspic (gelatin) which can be sliced and served as cold cuts together with other dishes.

1 complete sheep's head	2/3 tsp ground black pepper
2 large shallots finely chopped	or Szechuan pepper
2 cloves of chopped or crushed garlic	½ tsp red pepper
4-5 cups water	⅓ tsp turmeric powder
	salt to taste

First take the sheep's head outside and singe all the hairs over a fire. Be sure to singe it completely all around. Then take a dull knife and scrape the singed hair completely off. Then rinse, scrape more if necessary, and wash the head.

You may cut the head into large pieces, or you may want to cook the whole head. If you do want to cut it in pieces, be sure to tell any surrounding cowards not to watch this event.

You will get the best results by cooking in a pressure cooker. Put all the meat and water with the other ingredients and cook for 30 to 40 minutes over medium heat (this takes longer if you do not cut the head in pieces). You can add some other kinds of vegetables if you wish. Serve while hot.

GYUMA (Blood sausage)   serves 3-4

1 complete set lamb or goat's intestines	1 cup finely chopped onion
4 cups rice (or coarsely ground barley or wheat)	¼ cup finely chopped shallots
	1 tsp black pepper
2 quarts blood (4 pints)	½ tsp finely ground caraway seeds
2 lb ground beef (or use organs such as heart, liver, kidney, finely chopped)	½ tsp chili powder
	½ tsp Szechuan pepper
	salt to taste

Boil the rice or other grain until half cooked, and set it aside to cool. In a large bowl of any kind, mix the blood, meat, onion, and all the other spices. Sprinkle with a little flour and mix it well. Now add the rice to the blood mixture. (The rice must not be hot). Mix well. This mixture should be relatively runny, not firm like a dough. Salt to taste. Now set this mixture aside.

Wash the intestines thoroughly. You can wash the inside of the intestines by sticking one end to the tap and running water through. If you think it is not clean enough, cut the long intestine into shorter pieces and turn them inside out by looping them over your thumb.

Now, tie one end of the intestine with string. Use a pastry bag with a pipe. Fill this up with the mixed ingredients. Stick the pipe in the opened end of the intestine, holding it with your left hand, and gently squeeze the bag, letting the ingredients fill the intestine. If there are any clogs, stop and gently push the ingredients down with your fingers. DO NOT OVERSTUFF. Now tie the end tight with string.

In a large pot boil at least 2 gallons of water, then put the stuffed raw sausage in and cook for 5 minutes or so over high heat. (If the sausages do not fit, curl them up like snakes.) Then gently prick the boiling sausage with a toothpick in several places, to release the pressure. Continue to cook for another 20 minutes or more. This time puncture them deeper with a toothpick to see if they are done or not. If red blood is still shooting out, you need to cook them a little longer. Keep checking until no red blood appears. Now serve. You may serve whole sausages on a large plate, or you can cut them into smaller pieces and fry in oil and serve. Hot sauce (see p 92) can be served as a side dish.

NOTES. Commercial sausage casing can, of course, be substituted for intestines. If water is added instead of blood, use less and increase the amount of meat, to obtain a filling with the correct consistency. If blood is not used, the recipe is called *GYUKAR*, white sausage.

ༀ་ཁ་ཚ་

SHA KATSA (Spiced grilled meat, with sauce)

3 lb lean beef or lamb
½ cup chopped tomatoes
2 tsp hot chili
2 cloves minced garlic
1 medium size shallot, chopped

¼ tsp turmeric
½ tsp grated ginger
salt to taste
2 tbsp olive or vegetable oil
½ tsp dried green chives

Cut the meat into long strips about an inch wide. Then roast them over an open fire or a charcoal grill. Cook according to your taste: either well done, medium, or rare. Then cut the strips into smaller pieces about 2 inches long.

In a blender, put everything except meat, oil, and dried chives. Blend for about 2 minutes or until everything is mashed. Heat the oil and add the chives, quickly stir and take off the heat. Then add the mixture from the blender, stir and cook over high heat for about 1 minute. Now pour this whole mixture over the meat and mix it well.

You may sprinkle with chopped cilantro leaves (coriander) or green onion as a garnish.

 শ্রম্দুর্

SHAMDUR (Hot meat sauce)   serves 2-3

In Tibet there is a saying used as compliment: *Che yang mik dro chesong*, meaning 'I almost swallowed my tongue along with this sauce', it is used to tell a cook how delicious you think his sauce is.

½lb lean dried beef or unsalted beef jerky	2 tsp soy sauce
1 medium size tomato	3 tsp oil
2 tsp chili	¼ tsp fenugreek seeds
2 cloves minced garlic	½ cup chopped onion
	salt to taste

Toast the jerky slightly over the fire. Let it cool, then pound it in a mortar; or you can use a hammer to pound it on a chopping board. Pound it as finely as possible. Set it aside. Boil the tomato for 2 minutes. Then throw it into a blender, add chili, garlic, salt, and soy sauce, and blend for 2 to 3 minutes or until completely pureed. Pour the mixture over the powdered jerky and mix well. Then add a little hot water and mix well. Heat the oil and brown the fenugreek seeds, and then slightly brown the onion and pour into the mixture. Stir well and serve.

This sauce can be served with rice, bread, or any other main dishes.

 སེ་པན་དམར་འདྲུར་

SIPEN MARDUR (Hot sauce)

1 medium size tomato
3 tsp red pepper
1 cup plain yoghurt
3 cloves minced garlic

1 tsp minced ginger
salt to taste
½ cup chopped cilantro
    leaves

Boil the tomato with its skin for 2 minutes. Put it in a blender along with red pepper and yoghurt. Blend for 2 to 3 minutes. Now add the garlic and ginger, and salt to your taste and blend for another 2 minutes. Add finely chopped cilantro (coriander) leaves and stir well. Chill for half an hour.

This sauce is served just like the hot meat sauce (see p 91) with rice, bread, *momo*, *trimomo*, and so on.

Dairy Products

Since dairy products are used a lot in Tibet, and have some distinctive features there, I have included this little section on how we make butter, yoghurt, etc.

People ask me whether there is anything special and different about the taste of *dri's* milk. My answer is that *dri's* milk is much richer than cow's milk because it contains more butterfat.

One big change for anyone coming out of Tibet into the western world is in the number of different cheeses available. Of course I have been eating many kinds in the States which were quite strange to me at first. Those which are most like what we know in Tibet are Limburger, which is something like *churul* or *shosha* (see recipe for *Pagma*, p 76), and cottage cheese, which is similar to *Chura loenpa*, (p 96).

Draining the whey from sacks full of buttermilk; part of the process for making
Chura loenpa *(page 96)*

SHO (Yoghurt)

The way of making yoghurt in Tibet is like that in other countries. It is an important food for Tibetans. We use it in cooking and (if made from raw milk) for making butter; and it is a traditional party snack. In Tibet the milk used to make yoghurt may come from a cow, a *dri* (yak), or a *dzomo* (yak-cow hydrid), depending which is available.

2 gallons whole raw milk*
2 cups yoghurt (made from whole raw milk if possible)

Boil the milk for 2 minutes. Let it cool to around 80° (25°C). Add yoghurt to the milk and stir in well. Cover and wrap with warm blankets or towels. Put it in a warm place in your house, where the temperature is around 75°F (23°C). Let it sit there for at least 10 to 12 hours, or longer. It should turn into yoghurt. You can eat it plain or use it as an ingredient in sauces like *Sipen mardur* (p 92).

You can also make yoghurt in quantities smaller than those mentioned above.

* Yoghurt can be made from homogenized milk, but this yoghurt can not be used to make butter (for which only yoghurt made from whole raw milk is suitable). The culture can be started with yoghurt made from non-fat milk, if whole milk yoghurt is not available.

མར་

MAR (Butter)

In Tibet, butter is often stored in a goat's hide container. The skin is made wet before the butter is put in it. Then the skin shrinks and gets tight as it dries. This way there is no space for air, and the butter does not go bad. Butter can be stored this way for a long time. These containers are made in many sizes. The goat's hair is on the outside of the bag.

In some homes, butter is made by filling a big skin bag full of cream. Then the bag is stitched up tight and the children play with it. They roll it or kick it or punch it all around the house. Older people do this too.

2 gallons whole milk yoghurt or whole milk.*

Churn yoghurt or milk 1-15 minutes. (See the illustration of a Tibetan churn.) The bits of bubble-like butter will float to the top. Wash your hands and sprinkle one cup of cold water on the top of the yoghurt. Use your hands to gather the floating butter. Make it into a ball by squeezing it gently. Churn some more and add more cold water. It may take longer each time to get the butter. Continue doing this until no more butter floats up.

A residue of thin buttermilk will be left in the churn. We call this *dara*. You can drink it plain, or mix it with *tsampa* and eat it.

NOTE. You can use a blender set at low speed to make butter. An egg beater, electric mixer, and a wire whisk (if you are strong) will also work.

* Only yoghurt made from whole raw milk can be used for making butter.

ཕྱུར་བ་རྗེན་པ་

CHURA LOENPA (Soft cheese)

Chura is an important part of Tibetan cooking. Children and adults love to chew on *chura,* especially the kind with butter and sugar in it. The little chunks of dried hard cheese last a long time when you chew on them and they are eaten just as we eat candy in western countries.

To make cheese take the *dara* or buttermilk left over from making butter and boil it for 5 minutes. Let it cool down to 70°F (20°C) or less. It will separate into soft curds and a thin milky liquid, which is the whey. In Tibet the curds are called *chura loenpa* or *ser.*

Strain the whey off and use it for baking or give it to your livestock. In Tibet, we drain the whey off by pouring in into sacks and hanging them on poles or trees near the house (as shown in the drawing on page 93).

In Tibet most people do not add anything to the curd. They either eat it soft, calling it *chura loenpa,* which is like cottage cheese, or they just shape the curd and dry it. But you can add melted butter and sugar to the curd and mix it well. Then you can shape this into all kinds of things — round balls, flat wafers, even little beads. These little cookies are put out in the sun to dry or you can dry them in the oven on low heat. When it is dried it is called *chura kampo* which means hard dried cheese.

Ser or curd is sometimes squeezed through a small hole in a leather bag. When it is dried this way it looks something like noodles.

Another way is to squeeze a handful of curd out through your fingers. The shapes that come out are dried. Or the curd can be brushed from one hand by the other to make small granular pieces. This is sometimes ground even more when it is dried. Then it is called *chur ship* or ground cheese.

སྦ་

PAP (Tibetan yeast)

There are legends about how yeast was made for the first time, and some people today say yeast ought to be made the same way, the old way. But that would require ingredients such as eagle shit, the dried blood from a *drong* (wild yak), the tail of a jackal, and similarly inaccessible things. They do not really seem to be necessary after all.

1 cup millet flour
2 tsp powdered sugar
2 tsp finely ground brewer's yeast (or *pap*, if you already have some)
1/2 cup sheep's feet broth (as in Tibet) or lean beef broth or pig's feet broth.

Combine the millet flour, sugar and ground yeast in a bowl. Add the broth to these dry ingredients. Using your hands work it in to make a stiff dough. Roll the dough between your palms into a snake shape as thick as your thumb. Then cut this into pieces an inch long. Roll each piece into a ball and flatten it, just like a cookie. This will make it dry quickly.

Arrange dough patties in rows on a flat pan. Do not let them touch each other. Then cover them to make airtight. In Tibet we use fresh sage leaves for wrapping them up. A thick layer of leaves goes under the dough, then the dough is covered with another thick layer of leaves, and finally we wrap the whole thing with blankets or towels to keep warm. Put the wrapped pan in a warm part of your house (suggested temperature 85°F/29°C). It takes at least 48 hours for the dough to turn into yeast.

Open it after two days and you should be able to smell the fermentation. Remove the coverings and dry the yeast in the shade, never in the direct sun or in the oven. When it is dried, you can store it in an airtight container until needed for making *chang* (see recipe, p 54). *Pap* is only used for making *chang*, not for baking.

Some Recipes
Adopted By Tibetans

Over many centuries Tibetans have gradually absorbed or adapted recipes from outside Tibet.

The situation is different from that in most parts of the world, where adopted recipes may come from 10,000 miles away, and things like pizza make big jumps, from one continent to another. In Tibet we have only taken recipes from our neighbours. This is because we have only certain ingredients, which they often have also; and because Tibet has never been wealthy enough to import foods from afar.

So our adopted recipes are mostly Nepalese, Indian, Chinese etc. Traditionally, there have always been communities from these countries in our capital, and this has helped to introduce us to their dishes. Sometimes we cannot be quite sure where a dish originated, and it is anyway true that similar dishes can evolve in different places. But in my opinion it is generally correct to give the label 'adopted' to the receipes in this little section, and their mostly 'foreign' names support this view. I include them because they are popular among my people and one has to know about them in order to have a full picture of Tibetan foodways.

སྲན་མའི་འཁུར་ར།

SEME KHURA (WO) (Split pea pancake)

This dish is prepared mainly in the southern part of the country along the Nepalese border, and also in Lhasa. It was originally adopted from Nepalese merchants.

2 cups yellow or green split peas
2 cloves chopped or crushed garlic
1 tsp crushed or powdered ginger
2 medium sized shallots, finely chopped

¼ tsp turmeric powder
⅓ tsp cumin powder
⅓ tsp hot red pepper
salt to taste
2 tbsp flour
½ cup chopped onion
4 tbsp butter/cooking oil

Soak the peas overnight, or at least 8 hours, in a generous quantity of warm water.

Rinse the peas several times, then put them in the blender along with all the ingredients except the flour, onion and oil. Blend until pureed, then add water to blend the batter, which should be just like a pancake batter. (Blend 1 cup at a time if your blender won't hold it all at once.) Pour into a large bowl, add the onion and flour, and beat well. If the batter appears too thick or too runny, add more water or flour. Make sure the batter is just like your regular pancake batter.

Heat the griddle (you can use a frying pan) very hot at first. Pour just ½ a teaspoon of butter into the middle of it, and spread it around. Pour the batter (about ½ a cup) into the middle. Spread it until it is nicely flat and round; you can use a spoon to shape it. Once the batter is poured, lower the heat immediately. Cook for 2 to 3 minutes on each side, or until you think it is done. Repeat the same process until all the batter has been made into pancakes. Serve while hot.

In Tibet we use pulse or split pea of any kind. If you substitute lentils for the split peas, after soaking overnight you have to rub the lentils between your hands to remove the skin, and rinse many times until all the skins are removed.

We also add ground meat at the center of the pancake. First, prepare small patties of ground meat that are smaller in diameter than the pancakes, and pressed very thin; or use ground meat which has previously been sauteed until brown. You may add spices or chopped onions to the meat. There are then two ways of adding this meat filling. The first method of adding the meat is to start a pancake frying on the griddle, hollow out its top center portion with a spoon, add the uncooked meat patty, and cover the griddle with a cover that will trap the steam inside until both pancake and meat are cooked through.

The second method is to start two pancakes on an open griddle, fry them on one side until they are cooked enough to be ready to flip over (as you would with an American breakfast pancake), then add a spoonful of cooked meat on top of one pancake, and flip the second one on top of it to make a sandwich with the meat inside. Both pancakes should still be runny on enough on top when the meat is added that they can melt together. Fry, flipping over as needed, until cooked through.

The griddles we use in Tibet are mostly made out of thick clay, or even a piece of flat stone. They have covers made from clay. The cover helps it to cook evenly.

སྱུར་ཚོས།

KYURTSE (GUNDRU) (Pickled vegetable greens)

In Tibet the farmers pickle and dry these greens in large quantity during the late summer months to use in the winter, or to trade with nomads for their product. This is a typical dish of the Newar people of Nepal, which has spread to Tibet.

large quantity of mustard greens
   or radish greens
   or the two kinds mixed
1 large jar with airtight lid

Wash the greens thoroughly, and dry in the sun until they wilt. Pound or smash the greens evenly. You can use a rolling pin to roll the greens, or you can just use your palms to crush them. Whichever you do, do not let the juice escape. Put the greens in the jar by stuffing tightly. Make sure you press down hard so that they are well squeezed in. Cover the lid tightly, and set the jar in the direct sun for at least two to three weeks. If there is not enough sunlight, this can be done in a room at a temperature of 75°-80°F (24°-27°C).

   Open the jar and dry well in the sun. You can then use the dried greens to mix with any vegetable dishes. They will give you a slightly sour flavor when cooked with other ingredients, like meat or potatoes. The flavor gives you a good appetite.

ཚེར྄ཷཚེར྄ད།

CHOW-CHOW (Fried noodles with vegetables and meat)

This is a very special dish which is served only on special occasions, and is commonly served in modern Tibetan restaurants outside the country. However, it is clear from the name that the dish originated in China.

1 lb egg noodles	½ lb lean beef, lamb, or other
salt to taste	meat, cubed
½ stick (2oz : 60g) butter	1 tsp minced ginger
2 tbsp vegetable oil	2 tbsp soy sauce
1 large sliced onion	2 large sliced tomatoes
2 cloves crushed garlic	½ cup chopped green onion

Boil the noodles with a dash of salt. When done, drain the water and add half of the butter. Mix thoroughly to prevent sticking. Heat the oil, add sliced onion and garlic, and stir until browned. Add the meat, with the ginger, soy sauce and salt to taste. Saute for 10-15 minutes. Add tomatoes and stir and set aside.

In a frying pan, heat the remaining butter and pan-fry the noodles (ie fry without stirring until the bottom noodles are brown and crispy). You may serve all the noodles on one large plate, or separate helpings on individual plates. Pour the sauteed meat and vegetable mixture over the noodles, and sprinkle with finely chopped green onions.

ক্ট্রম্'

GYATUK (Noodle soup)   serves 3-4

1 lb flat egg noodles	salt to taste
2 tbsp oil	7 cups water
½ tsp fenugreek seeds	3 whole eggs
3 cloves minced garlic	1 cup chopped green onion
1 tsp ground ginger	or cilantro
2 lb diced lean beef or lamb	½ cup thinly sliced white
½ tsp cumin	onion,
¼ tsp turmeric	½ cup thinly sliced tomatoes

Heat the oil and add the fenugreek seeds. Stir until they are dark brown then add the garlic and ginger. Stir. Add the meat and other spices and stir again. Add salt, cover, and cook over low heat for 5 minutes or so. Add 7 cups of water and cover and cook for another 10 minutes.

In another pot boil water. Add the noodles and boil until done. Drain off the water and put some butter or oil on the noodles and mix it up well. This will keep them from sticking together. Beat the eggs up and fry them in very thin layers in a pan. It is better to fry half of them at a time. Cut the fried eggs into one inch squares.

Half fill each bowl with noodles. Cover the noodles with a ladleful of soup. Around the edge of the bowl arrange sprinklings of egg, chopped green onion or cilantro, or other relishes like the thinly sliced white onion and tomatoes. Serve with hot sauce (see pp 91-2).

SURU (Deep-fried meat soup)

This dish is well known in Lhasa and along the border towns of Tibet and China. It is no doubt adopted from a Chinese dish. In Tibet we sometimes add Chinese rice noodles (*phing*) to it.

2 lb beef (chuck roast or similar cut)	salt to taste
	2 eggs
1 stalk celery, cut crosswise	¾ cup flour
2 tbsp soy sauce	2 cups vegetable oil
1 tsp black pepper or szechuan papper (yerma)	

Boil the whole chunk of meat in about 5 cups of water.* To make the soup stock, add everything except the flour, oil and eggs, and cook for 15-20 minutes, or until the meat is done.

Beat the eggs in a bowl. Then add flour and a little water, and make a batter just like you would do for pancakes.

Take out the meat and let it cool. Meanwhile, heat the oil. Now dice the meat into bite-size cubes. Dip the cubes into the batter and deep fry them. Put them back into the soup stock and serve in bowls while hot.

* You can add additional water if you prefer to have a thinner soup. You can also add other vegetables such as carrots, mushrooms, radish greens, etc.

TRINRU (Steamed rice with meat)

In Tibet pork is normally eaten only in a few areas. Since this dish originated in China, the meat is normally pork. But the choice of meat is wide open. For instance, you might use bacon strips, or whatever is convenient. The recipe, which is unknown among the nomadic and farmer communities, was given to me by a former upper-class resident of Lhasa.

1½ cups rice	½ cup finely chopped celery
1 lb beef or any meat, thinly sliced and cut into strips	½ cup finely chopped onion
	2 tbsp soy sauce
	salt to taste

Boil the rice just as you normally do. Add the celery, onion and soy sauce, and salt to your taste. Mix well. In a large bowl (big enough to hold all the ingredients), lay out all the strips of meat evenly. Pour the rice into the bowl and press gently all around.

Set the bowl inside a covered steamer, and steam for 10-15 minutes. Take it out and flip the bowl over onto a large plate, tap it all around, and lift the bowl off. Now you have a nice round pile of rice with meat slices covering it all around. Serve while hot.

ལུག་ཤའི་གོབ་ཚེད།

LUGSHAE GOPTSE (Lamb or mutton curry)

In Tibet there is not always a great variety of spices, and some are not available to make a complete curry. Still, we made curry using whatever spices or ingredients were available locally. For instance, we might make a lamb curry by simply having meat and a few of these ingredients and spices.

This recipe originated in India. When making it, you can substitute any kind of meat for lamb, and other vegetables for carrots and green pepper. If you do so, then you have to name the dish after the meat, for instance, rabbit-curry.

2 lb lamb, diced to about bite size	1 tbsp oil
⅓ stick (1⅓ oz) butter	½ tsp fenugreek seeds
½ tsp cumin powder	½ cup chopped onion
⅓ tsp powdered chili pepper, or to taste	2 large chopped shallot
⅓ tsp turmeric	2 cloves crushed garlic
1 tsp crushed or ground ginger	2 large carrots, finely sliced
	1 cup chopped tomatoes
	½ cup sliced bell pepper

In a bowl, mix all the spices (except the fenugreek), butter, and meat together well. Let it blend for an hour or two. Heat the oil, add the fenugreek seeds, and stir until the seeds are dark brown. Add the onion, shallot, and garlic, and stir until browned. Add the meat, and sauté over a medium heat. Add the carrots and tomatoes and some water, stir well, cover, and cook for 10-15 minutes, or until the meat is nice and tender. Finally, add sliced bell pepper; mix and cook for 2 more minutes. Serve while hot with rice, *kapse*, (p 68), or other breads or vegetables.

CHUMI (Sweet rice dessert)

In Tibet we have a limited variety of dried fruits and nuts, and therefore we use raisins. We do not usually eat desserts as in N America and Europe; however, this particular rice dish became one which we eat after, or even before, the main course. It was evidently adopted from China.

You can add any dried fruits and nuts of your choice along with the raisins. If you can not find split rice, you can just use regular rice.

1 cup split rice	⅓ cup sugar or honey
½ stick (2oz / 60g) butter	½ cup raisins

Heat a frying pan and toast the rice slightly. Boil the rice just like you would normally do. Add butter and sugar and mix well.

In a large bowl, lay out the raisins evenly. Pour the rice into the bowl and gently press it down. Steam the rice in the bowl for 5 to 10 minutes. Take the bowl out of the steamer, and flip it over a onto a large plate. Tap around the bowl, and lift it off. Now you have a nice round outside pile of sweet rice covered with cooked raisins. You may serve this as a dessert.

ཡོལ། (ཀུ་སུ་མ)

YOLA (HALUVA) (Halva, a sweet pastry dessert)

Judging from its name, this is a Middle Eastern recipe that may have reached Tibet by way of India or Kashmir. This type of dish is very popular in Tibet, especially for baby food. In places where sugar and cardamom are not available we just use butter, flour, water and little salt.

½ cup whole wheat flour
½ cup white flour *
½ cup butter

3 tbsp brown or white sugar
½ tsp finely ground cardamom
    seeds
½ cup water

Heat the butter. Add the sugar and cardamom and stir well; then add both kinds of flour* and mix well, using a wooden or good solid spoon. Add water and again stir well, almost like kneading a dough over a medium heat. Cover and lower the heat. Cook for 10-13 minutes with ocassional stirring. Serve while hot.

* You may also substitute rice flour.

TIBETAN SOURCE MATERIAL

GLOSSARY

INDEX

Tibetan Source Material

Stories of the origins of food in Tibet are found in some Tibetan books. According to the most widely-known story, before people lived in Tibet, the Bodhisattva Spyan ras gzigs (Avalokitesvara) appeared on earth in the form of an ape, and went to Tibet to meditate. The female Bodhisattva Sgrol ma (Tara) took the form of a rock demoness and seduced him, and their children were the first Tibetans. From their father, the children inherited qualities like religious motivation and compassion; and from their demoness mother, they inherited fierceness, bravery, taillessness, and a love for eating meat. This was the origin of meat eating in Tibet. Later, either because they had passed beyond the ape stage and no longer knew how to gather wild fruit from the trees, or because there were so many of them that they had eaten it all, they began to starve. Their ape-Bodhisattva father gave them five kinds of grain — barley, wheat, rice, sesamum, and peas — and showed them how to plant and cultivate it, and this was the beginning of grain agriculture in Tibet. Different versions of this story are found in many Tibetan histories, including the *Blon po'i Bka' thang*, Don dam Smra ba'i Seng ge's *Bshad mdzod Yid bzhin Nor bu*, and Dpa' bo Gtsug lag 'Phreng ba's *Chos 'byung Mkhas pa'i Dga' ston*.

Other legends tell of the origins of Tibetan beverages. The eighteenth-century writer Bstan dar Lha ram, in his commentary on the monastic tea ceremony *Ja mchod kyi Dka' 'grel* relates a legend of an early Tibetan king who was suffering from an incurable illness. One day while he was resting on the roof of his castle, a bird flew overhead and dropped a leaf in his lap. The king put the leaf in boiling water, drank the beautiful-colored beverage that resulted, and was cured. He sent his ministers out in search of the plant that produced the miraculous leaves, which they discovered in China, and began to import tea to Tibet. Although tea was known in Tibet at least by the eleventh century AD, the Second Dalai Lama is said to have begun the practice of importing special high-quality tea from China for religious ceremonies in the early sixteenth century.

The anonymous book *Debate Between the Tea and Beer Goddesses (Ja Chang Lha mo'i Rtsod gleng Bstan bcos)* depicts a hilarious battle between the two beverages. The Goddess of Tibetan beer (*chang*) claims descent from the grains planted by the ape-Bodhisattva, and describes her historical connection with the great religious kings of the past and with important religious teachers like Milarepa. She denounces tea as a 'tramp of a drink' and 'Chinese devil masquerading as a beverage', and a 'bloody-colored religion-destroying drink', and demands that

the king of Tibet banish tea from the country. The tea Goddess
responds by claiming descent from the heavenly Wish-granting Tree
and the tree under which Buddha sat when he reached Enlighten-
ment, calls beer a 'sour-tasting witch of darkness', and in turn
demands that beer should be banished. From this relatively polite
beginning, the debate quickly degenerates into wild accusations and
some of the most colorful swearing and name-calling that one could
find in any language. Finally, the king settles the debate by ruling
that both goddesses will have to pay a fine for their tall tales and
excessive language; and he decrees that Tibetans will continue to
enjoy both beverages.

Glossary

This is in two parts. The first gives English: Tibetan as transcribed by the author: Tibetan script. The second gives Tibetan as transcribed by the author: Tibetan as transcribed by the Wylie system: English. For systems of transcription see the Notes which immediately precede the Foreword at the front of the book.

Words in parenthesis are alternative names. Where the author gives alternative transcriptions these are separated by slashes.

1. ENGLISH TO TIBETAN

English	Tibetan (as transcribed by the author)	Tibetan script
baking soda	bultok	བུལ་ཏོག་
barley	ne	ནས་
beef	langsha	གླང་ཤ་
	(chesha)	(ཆེ་ཤ་)
beer	chang	ཆང་
bell pepper	sipen ngonpo	སི་པན་སྔོན་པོ་
black pepper	fowarilbu	ཕོ་བ་རིལ་བུ་
blood	thrak	ཁྲག་
bone	ruepa	རུས་པ་
brown sugar	buram / goram	བུ་རམ་
buckwheat greens	drawoe loma	བྲ་བོའི་ལོ་མ་
	(yaba)	(ཡ་བྲ་)
butter	mar	མར་
buttermilk	dara	དར་
cabbage	logo petse	ལོ་ཁོ་པད་ཚལ་
caraway seed	goe nye	གོ་སྙེད་

cardamom	sugmel	སུག་སྨེལ།
cheese, soft	chura lonpa	ཕྱུར་བ་རློན་པ་
churn	dhongmo	མ་དོང་མོ།
cilantro (coriander)	sona pentsom	སོན་པ་བཙོམ་
corn	mamoe lotok	མ་མོས་ལོ་ཏོག
	(makey)	(སྐུ་ཀེ་)
cumin seed	zeera	ཟི་ར་
egg	go nga	སྒོང་ང་
farmer	shingpa	ཞིང་པ་
fenugreek	meeti	མི་ཏི་
flour	droship	གྲོ་ཞིབ་
	(droshe)	(གྲོ་ཞི་)
fruit, dried	shingtog kampo	ཤིང་ཏོག་སྐམ་པོ་
garlic	gogpa	སྒོག་པ་
ginger	gamug	ས་སྨུག
green onion	tsong ngonpo	བཙོང་སྔོན་པོ་
honey	drangtsi	སྦྲང་རྩི་
intestine	gyuma	རྒྱུ་མ་
lamb	lugsha	ལུག་ཤ་
lung	lowa	གློ་བ་
meat	sha	ཤ་
milk	homa	འོ་མ་
millet	thre	ཁྲེ་
	(gyakar)	(རྒྱ་དཀར་)
mortar and pestle	tun dang tunkhung	གཏུན་དང་གཏུན་ཁུང་།
	(dhotsom)	(རྡོ་ཚོམ།)
mushroom	shamo	ཤ་མོ་

mustard greens	petse	པེ་ཙང་།
	(yungkar)	(ཡུངས་གར་)
nettle	safo	ཟྭ་ཕོ
nomad	drogpa	འབྲོག་པ
nutmeg	zati	ཛ་ཏི
oil	noom	སྣུམ་
onion	tsong	བཙོང་
pea	ghum	སྲན་མ་
	(senjang)	(སྲན་ལྗང་)
pepper, black	fowarilbu	ཕོ་བ་རིལ་བུ
pepper, red	sipen marpo	སི་པན་དམར་པོ
pepper, Szechuan	yerma	ག་ཡེར་མ་
potato	shogog	ཞོགས་ཁོག་
potato, Tibetan sweet	droma	གྲོ་མ་
radish	lafug	ལ་ཕུག
radish greens	lafug ngotse	ལ་ཕུག་སྔོ་ཚོས།
raisin	gundrum	རྒུན་འབྲུམ་
red pepper	sipen marpo	སི་པན་དམར་པོ
rice	dre	འབྲས་
roasted grain	yoe	ཡོས་
salt	tsha	ཚ་
shallot	tsong gog	བཙོང་སྐོག
soy sauce	jangyul	ཇང་ཡུལ་
steamer	mogtsag	མོག་ཚགས།
	(mogtroe)	(མོག་ཏྲོལ་)
sugar, brown	buram / goram	བུ་རམ་
Szechuan pepper	yerma	ག་ཡེར་མ་

tea	cha / ja	ཇ་
tomato	tomato	ཀྲོ་མེ་ཀྲོ
tsampa (barley flour)	tsampa	རྩམ་པ
tumeric	gaser	སྣ་སེར
turnip	nyungma	ཉུང་མ།
	(yungma)	(ཡུང་མ།)
vinegar	kyurchu	སྐྱུར་ཆུ
water	chu	ཆུ
yeast	pap / phap	ཕབ
yoghurt	sho	ཞོ་

2. TIBETAN TO ENGLISH

Tibetan (as transcribed by the author)	Tibetan (by the Wylie system)	English
bultok	bul tog	baking soda
buram / goram	bu ram	brown sugar
cha / ja	ja	tea
chang	chang	beer
chesha	che sha	beef
chura lonpa	phyur ba rlon pa	soft cheese
chu	chu	water
dara	da ra	buttermilk
dhongmo	mdong mo	churn
dhotsom	rdo tshom	mortar and pestle
drangtsi	sbrang rtsi	honey
drawoe loma	bra bo'i lo ma	buckwheat green
dre	'bras	rice

drogpa	'brog pa	nomad
droma	gro ma	Tibetan sweet potato
droshe	gro phye	flour
droship	gro zhib	flour
fowarilbu	pho ba ril bu	black pepper
gamug	sga smug	ginger
gaser	sga ser	turmeric
ghum	sran ma	pea
gogpa	sgog pa	garlic
gundrum	rgun 'brum	raisin
gyakar	rgya dkar	millet
homa	'o ma	milk
jangyul	jang yul	soy sauce
lafug	la phug	radish
lafug ngotse	la phug sngo tshas	radish greens
langsha	glang sha	beef
logo petse	lo kho pad tshal	cabbage
lowa	glo ba	lung
lugsha	lug sha	lamb
makey	sma ke	corn
mamoe lotok	ma rmos lo tog	corn
mar	mar	butter
meeti	mi ti	fenugreek
mogtroe	mog khrol	steamer
mogtsag	mog tshags	steamer
ne	nas	barley
noom	snum	oil
nyungma	nyung ma	turnip
pap / phap	phab	yeast

petse	phe gang	mustard greens
ruepa	rus pa	bone
safo	zwa pho	nettle
senjang	sran ljang	pea
sha	sha	meat
shamo	sha mo	mushroom
shingpa	zhing pa	farmer
shingtog kampo	shing tog skam po	dried fruits
sho	zho	yoghurt
shogog	zhogs khog	potato
sipen marpo	si pan dmar po	red pepper
sipen ngonpo	si pan sngon po	bell pepper
sona pentsom	so na pad tshom	cilantro (coriander)
sugmel	sug smel	cardamom
thrak	khrag	blood
thre	khre	millet
tomato	kro me kro	tomato
tsampa	rtsam pa	tsampa (barley flour)
tsha	tshwa	salt
tsong	btsong	onion
tsong gog	btsong sgog	shallot
tsong ngonpo	btsong sngon po	green onion
tun dang tunkhung	gtun dang gtun khung	mortar and pestle
yaba	wa sba	buckwheat greens
yerma	g-yer ma	Szechuan pepper
yungkar	yungs kar	mustard greens
yungma	yung ma	turnip
zati	dza ti	nutmeg

Index of Recipes

The index includes all recipe titles in both English and Tibetan; also some categories of recipe, such as Soups and Desserts, which are not chapter headings in the Recipe Section.